D1758446

TAMING THE
TRUANT MIND

How Mindfulness Will Free You from
Troublesome Thoughts and Emotions

kamontip evans

© Kamontip Evans, 2016

First published (print and electronic) in Great Britain
by Business & Careers Press in 2016,
www.businessandcareerspress.com.

All rights reserved. No part of this book may be reproduced or
transmitted in any form or by any means, electronic or me-
chanical, including photocopying, recording or by an information storage and retrieval system – except by a reviewer who
may quote brief passages in a review to be printed in a maga-
zine, newspaper or on the Web – without prior permission in
writing from the publisher Business & Careers Press, 48 Clare
Lawn Avenue, London SW14 8BG.

Although the author and publisher have made every effort to
ensure the accuracy and completeness of information con-
tained in this book, we assume no responsibility for errors,
inaccuracies, omissions or any inconsistency herein. Any
slights of people, places or organizations are unintentional.

Printed in Great Britain by CreateSpace

ISBN: 978-0-9561391-5-3

To mom and dad,
to all my meditation teachers
and to Vaughan, Mattana,
Sutida and Wachara

Contents

Cartoon illustrations by
Chailayap Chanyam,
www.rockydolly.co.th

About the author

Kamontip Evans is an independent consultant in stress management and a teacher of mindfulness meditation – see www.mindskills4life.com. She also writes a blog on mindfulness for The Huffington Post – at www.huffingtonpost.co.uk/author/kamontip-evans.

When a university lecturer and radio producer in her mid-twenties, she experienced a life changing event. Suffering from severe cramps, breathing difficulties and physical exhaustion, she attended an austere retreat in mindfulness meditation in south Thailand. She emerged renewed, reinvigorated and indescribably happy. She has since meditated regularly and been to many more such retreats in Thailand, India and the U.K.

Kamontip has a Bachelor's degree in Liberal Arts from Chulalongkorn University, Bangkok, Thailand, a Masters in Education from the University of Detroit, U.S.A. and a further Masters in the Psychobiology of Stress from Roehampton University, London, U.K. She was formerly head of the foreign languages department at Srinakarin-wirot University, Songkhla, Thailand.

She has lived in South-West London for over 30 years, is married with three grown-up children and is a keen photographer – view a selection of her work at www.instagram.com/mkamontip!

Introduction

There are times in life when you feel as if you are stuck in the doldrums, or worse, in a dark place. You are worried about those mistakes, bad decisions or negative thoughts that have left you feeling guilty, angry, sad or disappointed.

You may be frustrated at your present circumstances, fraught or simply discontented. This book explores the root of the problem and shows you how to deal more effectively with negative thoughts, feelings, perceptions and anger. It offers guidance and tips on breathing techniques and mindfulness meditation, with supportive information from recent studies.

Methods offered in this book are cost-effective and highly versatile, allowing you to practice at anytime and anyplace. With a bit of self motivation and effort on your part, in your own time and space, and at your own pace, they will help you build a better quality of life.

The techniques and methods in this book, based on applied Buddhist philosophy and mindfulness meditation, are non-religious and suitable for all to put into effect.

I would like to express my most sincere and deep gratitude to all my meditation teachers over the years, as well as to all those who have shared their life experiences with me. They have greatly enriched mine.

All names in the book have been changed to protect privacy.

1 About

the truant mind

"
I watch little clouds float idly by

While my mind drifts alongside
I gaze up at the dark, thunderous sky
And my mind adopts a melancholia
I hear the sound of a rhythmic song
My mind tap dances gleefully to the tune
And when I think of my loved ones
Happy smiles spread across my face
My mind imagines the worst
When I'm alone in the dark or afraid
The mind shifts, floats, flits and drifts
Always looking outwards and rarely at home
Confused and rudderless in the past and future
Letting the body wander aimlessly
Forgetting what needs to be done
In its ever-changing emotional state
The mind is lost in its thoughts
And then wonders where happiness is,

Kamontip Evans

The nature of the mind is to think. And think it does! About all sorts of things, but with an inclination towards trivial issues and negativity, at least as long as we are unaware of this and allow it. A preoccupied mind is laden with thoughts, feelings and emotions. It is dull and heavy and has no room for productivity or creativity. In its balanced state, the mind is clear and calm, like the surface of a still pond. But throw something into it and the commotion starts. Any intervention to stop the commotion and the ripples expand. We need to wait, observe and let the water settle and return to its natural, balanced state.

The mind is playing truant when it's all over the place and not at home in the body. We are unable to switch off our thoughts, and the mind gets lost in them – confused and lacking in understanding. It busies itself trying to fix the past and future so that it can be happy in both, but it forgets to be happy right now. The urge to be happy and to achieve something is powered by the brain's reward system. It gives us motivation and extra endurance and makes us feel more alive. But every time we come close to happiness by getting what we want, the mind moves the happiness goalpost a bit further ahead.

Thus, we continually need a bit more than what we have if we are to be satisfied. We look for people, entertainment and material things out there to top up our pleasure, but we never look into our mind to see what makes it truly happy. Sometimes it takes a large-scale disaster – a tsunami, a flood, an earthquake or severe weather conditions where lives and properties are destroyed – for us to realise that our current problems are minute in comparison. This suggests that the happiness we crave is subjective; we feel happier and more content when we believe that we are better off than others. Such happiness can go up and down. Real happiness is about a truly contented mind, a mind that no longer plays truant, a mind that has stopped yearning, a mind that understands things just as they are.

Truancy and its psychobiological impact

Like with any truancy, negative consequences may soon follow a truant mind. It leaves us distracted, restless and confused, and we are more likely to make mistakes and suffer the risks of ill health.

We think with our thoughts until these thoughts become us. Whatever thoughts we have, the mind fuels more thoughts, fires them up and becomes hooked – like Pygmalion to the statue that he had carved. We believe our thoughts, identify with them and get lost in them without realising that they are simply the creations of our own mind, a mind that flicks from one thought channel to the next faster than a TV remote control. Upsetting events are displayed, rewound and fast forwarded again and again, leaving us in emotional turmoil. The stress response is triggered into action, and hormones are released to prepare us for the instinctive 'fight or flight' mode: our heart beats faster, breathing becomes shallower and muscles tense up.

As our thoughts circle around the incident or the person who has upset us, emotions flare or dip. This can occur while we are sitting alone at home, recalling events and speculating 'what if it happens again?' Before we know it, we are lost in unproductive thoughts for hours. We have perceived the situation to be far more stressful than it really was. Much of the stress we experience comes from our own thoughts rather than from what has actually happened.

The mind, cluttered with thoughts, gets stuck and stressed. This stress affects the function of the two nervous systems: the sympathetic and the parasympathetic. Both systems are connected to the same organs – the heart, lungs and digestive system – but they have opposite impacts. When strong emotions arise, the sympathetic nervous system is in charge. Hormones such as noradrenalin, adrenalin and cortisol are released. The first two trigger an increase in heart and breathing rates; the latter, responsible for an increase in free fatty acids and glucose in the blood stream, is released thereafter. Our energy levels are therefore boosted, helping us to deal with stress. Other states of mind, such as anger, sadness, shock and even love, are reported to affect this combination of hormonal releases in different ways.

Watching a boxing match, for example, can trigger a stress response as we swing, duck, punch, push and kick along with the action. Football fans will recognise the intense emotions during a penalty shootout, how they grip their seats and almost forget to breathe. When their team wins, they shriek, clap, jump to their feet or hug the person next to them in a state of elation. When their team loses, however, there's gawping, silence, distress, anger and shaking fists. The anger may result in some supporters starting arguments with fans from the opposing team. All these strong emotions, whether positive or negative, activate the stress response.

When these intense emotions settle, the cortisol soon returns to its baseline as a result of the body's negative feedback mechanism. If a high level cortisol is released for a long period of time, it affects our mood, sleep and brain function, and it can put us at risk of depression. Other health risks from prolonged stress include heart disease, diabetes, weight gain and premature ageing.

When we are relaxed, however, the parasympathetic nervous system takes over. It stimulates digestion and the production of insulin to keep the levels of glucose down. The heart and respiratory rates also slow down to help the body conserve energy. Whilst the body is resting or sleeping, though, our mind and brain are not. They review our thoughts and past events. Hence, we have dreams and nightmares! We often wake up to the same agonising thoughts that we had before going to bed, and we now continue with them. Disrupted sleep due to nightmares has a negative impact on our brain function and memory. For better health, we need to watch our mind.

Who is responsible for this stress?

"She hurt my feelings."

"I can never forgive them for what they have done to me."

"The noise was driving me mad."

Yes, unpleasant people or unpleasant environments may be far from one's liking, but they are already gone – five minutes ago, an hour ago, yesterday or last year. Why do you continue to feel irritated by them? You have unwittingly pushed a 'save' button, thus recording them in your memory. Given that what is stressful can vary from one individual to the next, does your present pain actually come from what others did or said? Or is it just your perception or negative memory of it that is causing the pain?

If it's a perception, what then is perception? Perception is how we think or look at the world. If it's a memory, what is this memory, anyway? It is a thought about the past. In both cases, they stem from a thought. And what is a thought? It is something that arises naturally, whether or not we want to think it. It comes and goes of its own accord, like the air we breathe. Why then do we choose to look negatively at things, thus maintaining the memories that later torment us? This is partly because the mind has a tendency to dwell on unresolved issues or situations that ended unsatisfactorily. It will keep reminding us to do something about the past to make sure that the future will be better. A mind that lacks understanding is confused and unable to let go of anything that it is preoccupied with.

A lack of control is said to be one of the reasons why we are stressed. What exactly are we trying to control? Situations, circumstances, or people? – all of which are impossible, because they are in transient. Thus we are left with exhaustion. When things don't go as planned, we blame ourselves, others, situations, or equipment for the failure. We forget to look inward – at our own mind. It's as if we have an open wound on our hand and we massage our leg instead. We might feel more relaxed from the massage and forget about the wound on the hand for a while, but the wound remains untreated, and infection may flare up afterwards. It is easier to point fingers at others for our misery or seek external relief to distract us from the pain and help us feel better. If there is anything that needs to be kept under control, it's our own mind. Controlling the mind is not easy, either, because if you push it one way, it will try to squeeze out the other way. What we need do is to tame it so we can remain calm regardless.

Stress itself is not all bad. A short dose of it is found to help boost our immunity and sharpen sensory perception. It provides us with that extra 'oomph' and energy to get us out of bed in the morning. Faced with an approaching house fire, one manages to run away at a speed much faster than usual and may be able to lift heavy items with ease. Moreover, an increased stress hormone release keeps us alert and ready to face challenges. The brain becomes temporarily sharper and memory is enhanced, which is useful for exams or job interviews. Vocabularies that we don't normally use flow fluently from our mouth, especially when in a dispute! More importantly, stress also gives us a learning opportunity – to observe the mind and see what it is doing so that we know how to tame it better.

We may have mindlessly reacted to people and situations in the past, but we don't need to act that way anymore by minding our mind.

Identify your triggers

Imagine lying down, relaxing in peace. Suddenly there's a bonk. The mind leaps to that sound to investigate and returns to tell us whether it is likable, unlikable or whether we should do something about it or discard it. Normally we discard this random piece of information. If, however, something about that sound catches our attention, a train of thoughts follow, linking it to people or past events….. emotion arises. Memory is stored, forming a perception that we will base our future judgement on. If we interpret this hearing sensation wrongly, for example, we think it's an intruder when it was just the wind pushing a wooden spoon off the table. Fear arises. This biased perception can trigger a negative emotion and memories from the past – if we are unaware of what our mind is doing.

We may have some triggers that spark off negative thinking. Note down these triggers and how you react to them to help you see how they influence your thoughts, emotions, and actions. These can be the sight of someone who irritates you, looking after a new baby, fear of loneliness, having your views challenged in arguments, lack of respect from colleagues at work, an impossibly high workload, financial problems, etc. Rank them in order of importance (1-5).

Note down your reactions – for example, shouting, shaking, sulking, walking away, arguing, throwing things, smoking, drinking, snacking (1-5).

Choose one of the triggers above. Identify whether the trigger enters the mind through sight, sound, touch, taste, smell, or if it is your thinking about the past.

Write down your emotional response to this trigger. Know that this emotion is just a state of mind that arises in the mind, lingers on for a while, and disappears on its own accord.

Do any physical changes (e.g. heartbeat, breathing, temperature, facial expression) occur whilst you think about/recall this trigger? Note down these changes.

Note down any additional thoughts that follow this trigger.

How would you like to respond to this trigger in the future?

Now that you know what can push your buttons, be aware and beware of them. Remind yourself that these are merely triggers. If they prove to rouse a negative response, you can unlearn them.

The following chapters will show you how.

2 Educating the mind

"

It is the mark of an educated mind to be able to entertain a thought without accepting it,
Aristotle

To think or not to think

As children, we are taught to think and think harder – for thinking makes us clever. We think until we become excellent thinkers. Now we can't stop. Our thoughts seem to have a life of their own, flitting here and there – busily planning, calculating, analysing, judging, depriving us of sleep and beyond our control. The current educational system favours competitive hard work, with a wealth of knowledge to learn and memorise – a lot of which ends up being irrelevant to our working life. The same system fails to teach us how to silence the mind when abundant thoughts are not needed. A clouded mind cannot see the solution. All we get is a headache. Our society is full of thinkers whose over-thinking can lead to stress, depression, and neurosis. Not using one's head enough may also have a negative impact on neuronal connections, reducing one's brain power and memory function. By indulging in or pushing away certain thoughts, we are, in effect, giving them significance and allowing them to occupy our mind. We need to educate our mind to know how to think.

Thinking without awareness

Thoughts arise independently with or without us consciously thinking about them. We discard a lot of them automatically, but there are some that the mind seems to dwell on more often, partly because we are unaware that we are thinking and partly because they have not been resolved. As the old saying goes, the tongue will always return to a sore tooth. When someone upsets us, the thought of that person may occupy our mind all day without us realising it. If we realise that we are thinking, the thought process will come to a halt. But not for long. The mind soon returns to it again. The more we observe our thoughts, the more the mind comes to understand the nature of its own thinking, and it will be able to let go of those thoughts.

Thought seasoning

To make food more enjoyable to eat, we add seasonings: oregano, chilli, cumin, basil, pepper – maybe just a sprinkle of salt. Likewise, to make a thought more enjoyable, the mind seasons it and spices it with further thoughts and feelings, turning the thought equivalent of a lettuce leaf into a mixed salad. Emotion is thus fired up – making our thoughts more flavoursome, more 'more-ish', and more addictive. That's why some angry people say that they can't stop their anger because they enjoy it while they are at it. Adding past and future worries to our thoughts, and we are completely hooked. We eventually start to believe in our own concoctions – our own signature thought dish!

In a stormy relationship, it only takes a small argument and some thought seasonings to convince us that the other person is definitely in the wrong. One's partner, once the perfect one, can turn into a hideous monster whom one can barely set eyes upon, let alone be in the same room or share a bed with! When a negative thought arises, know that it is just a thought, nothing more.

We season our thoughts because we like or dislike what we see, hear, touch, taste, etc. We want more of what is pleasing and reject the displeasing.

The 'I want' thought

In this world there are only two tragedies. One is not getting what one wants, and the other is getting it,

Oscar Wilde

Reality TV competitions attract hundreds of thousands of candidates, seeking fame and fortune. The winner takes all – including the stress and strain of getting there and handling the subsequent fame. As the fame reaches its height, the desire to be famous then reverts back to the need for privacy, normalcy, and anonymity. What we want is sometimes contradictory in terms, because we have an incorrect mindset in the first place.

Getting one's own way boosts our ego, potentially causing resentment in others. Worse still, it contributes to selfishness and a narrow point of view. Beware of 'I want' and the consequences that follow.

I was eight when I cried for a pair of shiny red shoes with pretty red ribbons on them. I threw a tantrum when my parents said 'no'. At home, my father asked, 'Why do you want those shoes so much? You just got a black pair recently! Are those shoes really that wonderful?' 'Yes they are', I replied defiantly. 'Well, if they are wonderful enough to make you feel like you're flying, then I'll go and buy them for you right now', my dad said calmly. I thought about it. The shoes were very pretty but would they bring me enough uplifting joy to make me feel like I was flying? Could they? The answer was 'NO'. Realising the truth, I told my father that the shoes were not that wonderful, and I didn't want them anymore. Since then, whenever I want anything really badly, I ask myself whether the object is wonderful enough to make me fly. And pretty much all the time – it won't. I am forever grateful to my father for such an invaluable life lesson.

The 'I don't want' thought

We suffer from what 'I don't want' as much as what 'I want'. Not always getting what we want is a fact of life. We don't want to get old, but we are getting older everyday: cells in our body change and die all the time. We don't want the children to be stubborn, but they have their own ways of thinking and doing things. The list of what we don't want can go on and on. The longer our list, the more frustrated we get – forgetting that they are merely thoughts! What's more, what we want or don't want is transient and constantly changing. Who knows, things may change again. No need to get uptight about them.

The negative thought

It is said that the mind, like water, tends to flow downward – that it has a tendency to dwell more on the negative rather than the positive. Negative thoughts, much like drugs and alcohol, can be addictive and breed further negativity. Once they arise, these negative thoughts are registered on our mind as perceptions that will guide our future actions.

Bob, a professional cyclist, was in his late twenties. Prior to his leg injury, he excelled in cycling. After his recovery, Bob tried to get back into it but ended up with more injuries, resulting in a loss of confidence and a lapse into depression. His fulltime job also suffered setbacks due to the depression. He wanted to get back into cycling, as he knew he was capable, and if he could prove himself it would resolve a lot of his problems. *Every time he entered a race, his mind would return to his past injuries, and he was convinced that he would never make it back to the top. He came to see me to work on his confidence whilst working hard at his training.*

With his confidence back on track and with a fierce determination, he managed to come fourth in a competition. He was thrilled with his achievement. Bob admitted that towards the end of the race, he had a flash of fear about a possible leg injury, but this time he was able to let go of it quickly and carry on.

The obsessive thought

Obsessive thoughts can overpower us, contributing to a change in our behaviour and causing damage to our health. Obsession with weight, cleanliness, appearance, winning – can all bring about stress.

Gwen left an abusive man to start a new life in the UK. The memory of him haunted her constantly. There was sadness in her eyes and sadder was her smile. She couldn't stop thinking about the verbal abuse she had suffered. I asked her why she was still worrying about him when he was in another country, a long way away from her and with no financial means to follow her. She was completely safe from him. There was a long silence. She stared long and hard at me and said, 'Are you saying that I'm addicted to my own thoughts?'

I did not need to answer. Gwen found her own answer right there. And she knew it. A smile appeared at the corner of her mouth as her face brightened up. Her smile turned into a big grin.

Obsessive thoughts can even be tragic.

Some twenty years ago a local newspaper reported a story of a woman in her late 30s. How she loved having her photo taken every time she walked past a photo booth! If she didn't like the way she looked, she would have plastic surgery to perfect it. After each operation she felt a bit happier. Several operations later, she was despairing, convinced that she would never look good enough, and, sadly, she ended her life.

Watching and getting to know your thoughts

When we are worried, we want the situation to be resolved quickly. Sometimes, it's a good idea to simply wait and see how things unfold without seasoning, saying anything, or interfering. Like most good therapists would patiently listen to our woe, we need to develop patience to listen to our inner dialogue in our head from beginning to end without doing anything.

Know that real problem is not about the painful past or what's going to happen in the near future. It is your dwelling on it at this present moment. Such thought arises in the present, and you need to deal with the present occurrence by being your own trusted listener. When these troublesome thoughts and emotions are tended to and listened to with patience, they will naturally calm down.

The more you watch and observe your thoughts, you will see that there is an end to your thought process without you trying to get rid of or let go of it. Sometimes it ends before you even know it. That's the way it is. All we need do is to be aware of them and watch them.

Watching one's thoughts is different from thinking about them. Thinking requires you to become an active player. However, when watching your thoughts, you are playing the third person, looking and observing as your thoughts run past on your mental screen. You might feel some agony, as we all do, when we identify with the characters on the screen. Nevertheless, every time you watch it, the plot becomes clearer and more predictable – you even know the dialogue by heart and how it's going to end. Eventually you get bored stiff and don't want to watch it anymore. Likewise, the mind learns to know and understand the pattern of your own thoughts. The mind becomes streetwise with them and able to let go of them. The more you watch, the more you unravel or undo the power that pain and stress have over you. This can only happen if you are the watcher, not the thinker.

Understanding the written text above does not guarantee that you will stop dwelling on your thoughts or becoming efficient at handling them. The understanding must come from practising it. This is the key to managing your thoughts and safeguarding yourself from unnecessary stress. Here are some other ways to keep your thoughts more positive.

Thinking yourself happy

If our state of mind is dull and joyless, Venerable Arayawangso advises that we can adjust our mind and uplift our mood instantly by breathing in and out and making the mind happy.

Simply close your eyes. Take a deep, deep breath and make your mind happy. When you breathe out, make your mind happy again. Make your mind happy when you breathe in and when you breathe out. You will find that your lips automatically go into a smiley motion, making you instantly happy.

You may also try this. Take a deep, deep breath and recall a moment of happiness. Let this sense of joy permeate through your body, and then breathe out. Take another deep breath and now think of a peaceful memory, and let this peace and calm spread through every part of your body, then breathe out. You can do this anywhere and anytime.

Shifting your thoughts

In hospitals, play therapists keep young children's attention fixed on a toy or a game in front of them to shift their attention and minimise their fear of the injection. Stress comes when you let the mind out. When it does not remain in the vicinity of your body or the task in front of you, you are in trouble.

Some of you may have had the experience of giving a presentation in front of a large audience. You feel that all eyes are on you, judging you, inspecting you, and you may start feeling sick in your stomach – thinking that they might not like your clothes, your words, the sound of your voice ... Suddenly you start stammering and repeating yourself, forgetting your lines and then ... Your mind goes blank – all because you are focusing on everyone else in the room rather than on the speech you need to deliver.

Whatever you are doing, give that activity your full attention. Be with it. When you focus outward – there's housework to be done, overdue bills to be sorted, a lawn to be mown, a mess to clear up – the mind searches for things that need to be done and piles them up like a mountain. Twenty-four hours seems not long enough to tackle everything. Discouragement ensues. Once we get down to tackle those tasks, they are not as burdensome as our thoughts have made them seem.

Sometimes the problems picked up by the mind are not even real or relevant to the present. For example, you are about to nod off, and a murder case from a TV detective series pops up. The mind jumps to it and busies itself at resolving the case. An hour later you still lie there wide awake, trying to sort out who had done it.

Another effective method you can use is to shift your attention to body movements, thus reducing the activity of the amygdala, the emotional brain, making you calmer.

When you sit at a desk, snowed under by your workload, feeling stressed, shift your focus to body awareness for a brief moment. Be aware that you are sitting on that chair. Are you sitting comfortably? If not, adjust yourself accordingly. And while you are adjusting your position, be aware of your body movements, be they your arms, hands, neck, feet, your head tilting slightly backwards in a more comfortable position, your shoulders dropping, your facial muscles gently resting, your eye lashes slowly flicking as your breathing becomes deeper, slower, and more comfortable. Simply be aware of these little movements – to free your head from words and thoughts. Alternatively, you may want to get up and stretch your body. Once again be aware of your body movements when you stretch. Be fully with them.

Being selective with your thoughts

Too many thoughts lead to a lack of focus. Our ability to learn, sustain attention, and retain memory is reduced. When something has caught your attention, you stop, freeze-frame, and enlarge the message or picture like that on your smart phone. The thought seasonings will act as if you've opened up another collection of applications on your phone, as you zoom through page after page. Pick one thought that needs urgent attention, and focus on it fully. Stay with it until you resolve it, or limit yourself to spending just 10 or 15 minutes on it before moving on to your next thought. Do not allow yourself to ponder for longer than the time you set out to do this even if you still can't resolve it. When the mental task is over, take a deep, deep breath, think of a happy/joyful thought, and let this happy/joyful sensation spread through your body before breathing out. Do this a couple of times until you feel more relaxed. Make sure you select your thoughts wisely and for positive effect.

Letting your thoughts be at one with nature

Nature brings pleasure to the heart and soul. Studies have shown that nature can soothe pain and enhance brain function. The following exercise aims to help you connect with nature by shifting your thoughts.

Find an area in a quiet garden or park where you can sit safely and comfortably – preferably with light, gentle sunshine. Sit down and get yourself into a comfortable position. Take a few deep breaths, and let your eyes gently close. Continue breathing deeply, and with each out-breath let your body relax completely. Be aware that you are sitting on a bed of soft green grass or leafy carpeted earth. Feel that cool, solid sensation of the earth underneath you. Take a slow deep breath … take it all the way from the ground, and when you breathe out, let yourself become part of that earth. Carry on with more deep breaths until you feel firmly rooted to the cool earth – like a tree. Let yourself be at one with the environment, and enjoy that sensation. With each breath you take, you can feel the fresh, cool air softly entering your body, going all the way to your abdomen. As you breathe out, notice the warm air slowly moving upwards and finally passing through your nostrils. Repeat a few more times. As you continue to sit there comfortably, feel the sensation of the cool/warm air lightly caressing your skin: you are part of that air, let yourself be part of that air, as light and refreshing as that air. Let yourself be at one with nature … and enjoy! When you have had enough, take a few deep breaths, open your eyes and resume normal breathing.

Conveying positive energy with your thoughts

Thoughts are a form of energy that can affect their own creator as well as those nearby. Your strong, agitated thoughts can disrupt the harmony of a small gathering even if you remain entirely silent. Your positive, happy thoughts can help to energise an environment and the people around you. Peaceful, clear thoughts bring a calming energy to an environment. It is said that if you come face to face with a fearsome wild animal, it tends to attack the person with the most fearful thoughts first because animals can pick up on the sweat odour resulting from the release of stress hormones. A person's depressive thoughts can affect the thoughts and emotions of their spouse and their family members. Similarly, a parent's angry thoughts can negatively impact their child's behaviour.

In an office environment where daily disagreement prevails, antagonistic thought energy can spark off further disagreements. When stepping into an office, you may be able to sense discord or a negative vibe in the environment. It is unlikely that the business will flourish to its full potential in such a place. However, there is something you can do to tone down the negative thought energy. This starts with your positive thinking. With your positive thought energy, you can deal more effectively with others. To be able to send your thought energy, you need strength of mind, and this is obtained by having a clear, calm mind. Send your positive thought energy to troublesome colleagues in the form of loving kindness regularly (see Chapter 8).

Harnessing the power of thought

Studies show that a feeling of hopelessness can worsen one's ill health, whereas positive thinking helps with medical recovery. For better health, think more positively! The power of positive, imaginative thinking can be used to help young children conquer their fears and nightmares and thus sleep better.

Lily was five when she moved to a new school far from home. Being a new girl in class and with a long journey to school on public transport left her feeling anxious. She began having nightmares and recurring dreams about falling off a cliff and was scared of going to bed.

I asked her what would stop her from falling off the cliff. She said that it would help if she could have wings to fly. So we talked about putting wings on. I asked her to describe the wings she would like to have. She described the colours and texture of the wings. I told her that before she went to bed, she should be aware that she had those wings with her and whenever she felt that she was falling off the cliff, all she needed was to flap her wings and fly. I asked her to practise the scene of flying in her head just before bed. Lily had a lot of fun imagining the scene. The following morning, she said that she had that dream again but this time she was flying rather than falling. The following nights she described the wings in different colours and textures and seemed to have fun changing her wings. This went on for three nights before the nightmares disappeared, and her anxiety about the new school subsided.

Everything is transient – like our breaths that keep changing, in and out, short and long. Without those changes, we cannot survive. Worries are merely thoughts; no need to cling to them. And remember:

Your worst enemy cannot harm you as much as your

own thoughts, unguarded,

Lord Buddha

3 Understanding perceptions

When you take a photo of something, you look at your object from different angles – left, right, front, back, above, and below – to get your best shot. When looking at people and situations, why be so hasty to take a quick shot? Given that the sunlight and shadows change all the time, you need to make adjustments for your photoshoot. People and situations also change; we need to adjust our perception of them.

Perceptual errors

Developing the wrong thought pattern is like buttoning one's shirt. If we get the first one right, all will go accordingly; if we get the first one wrong, all the rest will go awry. It's important to get our thoughts on the right track from the start, because they will become our future reference.

Changing how we look at the world

We cannot change the past, but we can change the negative way we look at the past so that the mind will not hold on to bitterness. Changing one's perception is far better than suppressing one's feelings. The latter is like sweeping unwanted emotions that can't be dealt with under the carpet, leaving them to fester in your mind. The following scenario shows that by adjusting your perception, you will feel better:

Your football team's disappointing performance in the penultimate match of the season has left you feeling devastated. Everyone said your team was certain to win, but the result was a mere 0–0. You feel so let down – it would've felt just as bad if they'd lost! Your face drops, your body droops, and your shoulders slouch in disappointment. But when the sports commentator eagerly notes that your team was 'unbeaten', all of a sudden, you start to feel better. The word 'unbeaten' auto-

matically brings back a sense of pride. You are able to walk tall, with your head held high and a proud smile spreading across your face. One positive word in a disappointing situation, and your perceptions and mood can change completely!

A stressful situation can suddenly become silly, hilarious, touching, or joyful when you alter your perception. How many times in the past have we been annoyed with our parents when they tidied our room, or gave an opinion we didn't want to hear, or told us the same story over and over again? By adjusting the way we look at those situations, we would have discovered love, care, and kindness instead.

The perceptual illusion

The same sensory input can be interpreted in many different ways. When our perceptions are biased or distorted, we suffer. For example, what we have learnt and our state of mind influence how we perceive the world.

At a party, an attractive woman in a stunning floral dress caught Jack's attention. He approached her and complimented her dress, adding that it reminded him of his mother's beautiful curtains. Her smile froze. She stared at him with an indescribable expression and, without a word, walked away. Jack was astonished that his enthusiastic, well-meant comment was met with such a cold, negative reaction.

Her perception was based on the conventional idea that a curtain has its own place – not on her body! Therefore, having her dress compared to a curtain is not a compliment. Jack's genuine admiration was interpreted as insensitive and insulting.

Products that are repeatedly billed as 'must-haves' or 'to-die-for' make them seem more desirable. Add the words 'limited edition' and they sell like hot cakes. In and of themselves, these products are not at all 'must-have' items. But our distorted perception of reality makes us think otherwise. During a sale people queue overnight to buy the products, and fights have broken out over sold-out soft toys, handbags, or the last pair of high heels. If these items are truly must-haves and to-die-for, then their desirability should be timeless; but in reality some of them, especially fashion items, only last one season or until the launch of the next trend. Wear your to-die-for dress the following year, and you easily look dated.

Moreover, sex sells in advertising. A number of things become 'sexy' to the point of being absurd. Now we have sexy drinks, sexy perfume, sexy furniture, sexy hair, sexy shoes, etc. Is there such a thing as 'sexy shoes'? Walk in those high-heeled sexy shoes for a few hours and one starts to limp rather than be sexy. If one sexy hair falls into your soup, would you eat the soup and find it sexy still? Our misconceptions make these items more desirable than they truly are. Being sexy is not only over-rated but also hugely distorted. In reality, the human body excretes smells, there's grease on the hair, snot from the nose, wax from the ears, sleep from the eyes, plaque from the teeth, sweat from the skin, dirt under the nails, urine, and stools. Without a wash, the body oozes nothing but a pungent smell. We may try our best to decorate this body with fragrance, hairspray, and cosmetic paints, but then when our hair comes out in the shower and starts to clog up the drain; we don't even want to touch it.

Perception and cultural differences

Culture plays a part in shaping our views. We may appreciate and welcome other cultures, reject them, or regard our culture as superior. A lack of awareness of other cultures can lead to misperception. For example, Thai people often ask 'where are you going?' – meaning 'how are you?' Not knowing what this means, foreigners may perceive a Thai's friendliness as nosey. Similarly, in many Anglophone countries throughout Africa, the usual response to 'How are you?' is 'I am fine'. To other English speakers, this can sound slightly defensive, and people can incorrectly perceive this as rude.

In Japan, having a long neck was once considered beautiful because it looked good rising out of a kimono. In China, small feet used to be thought desirable – young Chinese girls went through a lot of pain wrapping up their feet to stop them from growing. In some cultures, long ears and big bottoms are the symbols of beauty. In the West, tanned skin is seen as attractive – hence the popularity of sun beds and fake tans. In the Far East, pale coloured skin is considered more attractive, so whitening cream is a must. These ideals are also changing over time. A few decades ago, the hourglass figure was considered attractive. Nowadays, lean and thin ladies seem preferable. Beauty really is in the eye of the beholder – if we were to put all the ideal beauty requirements from different cultures together, we'd end up with a weird-looking being!

What's more, we use words to label things, and we attach meaning to these words until a quarrel can sometimes break out. 'Is it a sliding door or a French window?' can easily become a topic of heated argument. An English dog says 'woof' or 'bow wow', while a Japanese dog says 'wan' and a Thai dog says 'hong' or 'bok'. When someone falls down from a tree, you may hear a 'thud', but Thais hear a 'tuub'. According to the part of the world we belong to, we may interpret and label these sounds differently. Differences in labelling sounds of nature may be amusing, but when it comes to views on the use of words which are deemed offensive, suddenly people start to react with anger rather than bemusement over which words are being used. The same word can be an insult, teasing, or endearing depending on who uses it, how they say it, what the context or situation is, and, most importantly, how the addressee perceives the word. In reality, words are just words. We make them up to communicate with each other. Yet we can argue like mad about who said what and why what they said hurt. As Antoine de Saint-Exupéry puts it in The Little Prince:

//

Words are the source of misunderstandings.

Given the perceptual differences, why do we hold on to our own particular perceptions as being the correct ones or the best? Why get agitated when people disagree with our views?

Each to his own perception

Whether a situation is problematic depends on how you choose to interpret it – as the following story illustrates.

Eleanor had moved to Uganda for six months on a project and had been enjoying the local food. One day, one of her colleagues saw her eating and said 'Hey, Fat lady! Keep eating!' Eleanor was stunned, but just nodded. Later, she spoke to another colleague about the incident, who explained to her that being called 'fat' was a compliment and a sign of being healthy. Her colleague was happy that she was enjoying the local food. Had she chosen to interpret the word 'fat' as an insult, she could have gained an enemy at work. However, she realised that her perceptions are not always correct and can actually cause unnecessary hurt.

Whatever perceptions we have, we can always find reasons to justify them and act on them. Perception provides a framework for our thoughts to build on. If we consider ourselves incapable, we may develop fear and a lack of confidence; if we perceive a task as impossible, we will stop trying and give up on it; if we perceive our job as boring, then there is a lack of incentive to carry on. When you don't like something or someone, you are likely to develop a negative mindset with regard to them, hold on to these perceptions, and proceed to find faults with them. For example, when at a restaurant you may find the choice of food isn't quite what you were looking for. The agitation you feel may cause you to find flaws with the food, the ambience, the service or the clientele, or you may even become annoyed with your companion. At the end you are convinced that the restaurant is a poor choice, because you started off with a negative perception.

Perceptions affect the way we care for each other

Caring for ageing parents with dementia can be difficult due to their unpredictable moods and changing behaviour. It is devastating to see the transformation of one's parents into such a state. If you perceive the situation as simply being hopeless, this makes it harder for yourself and for your parents – you may find yourself unable to cope. However, by changing your perception and viewing the dementia according to reality – your parent's ageing brain is shrinking in size and impacting their behaviour – you may be able to treat them with dignity, patience, kindness, and understanding. After all, if you were to suffer from a long-term, severe fragile health, your parents would probably do their utmost to care for you. With such hindsight, you may be able to face difficulties with care and a good sense of humour.

Perceptions can be exaggerated

The feeling of pain, for example, is not constant – even though it may seem that way when we have it. When we focus on the pain and perceive it to be unbearable, the pain intensifies, but when we stop thinking about it, it doesn't seem to bother us as much. The fear of pain makes it worse. Young children can be frightened of injections, but can be given coping strategies such as shutting their eyes tightly, counting from one to five forward and backward, or biting their teeth together and holding their mummy tight. They will then be able to handle the pain better, because they have shifted their focus to other senses or cognitive functions instead of the pain itself. They can apply this technique to combat future fear of pain and be more in control of their experiences. Their perception of pain is thus altered – even though they still feel the pain, it seems more tolerable.

When the attention is not focused on the pain, the perception of pain changes accordingly, as does the fear and the degree of pain.

Be aware and beware of your perceptions

We need to be aware and beware of our perception. Wrong perception can lead to wrong action. For example, your partner returns home, looking grumpy. If you take this personally and think he is annoyed with you for no good reason, you will get annoyed with him without knowing the true reason. Your perception leads you to jump to the wrong conclusion, and you may proceed to feel hurt and irritated and say something that makes things much worse. When you are aware of your own perception, you can put this feeling on hold. Remember: perceptions are perceptions, not an extension of ourselves! The next morning your husband may tell you what a dreadful day he had had at work, and you may be glad you took the precaution of your negative perception. Accumulated negative thoughts become distorted perceptions, which breed more negative thinking. If you are not happy, look again at how you perceive the world. Re-evaluate your perceptions and be aware of them, for a long-term negative perception that turns on oneself can lead to depression.

The process of perception is automatic and instantaneous. Reading about terrorism, crimes, wars, and disasters may turn our perception of the world sour. Reading gossip columns may be fun, but the write-ups may or may not be true. If we read them often enough, we may start thinking along the line of these sensationalist views and believing the nonsense. False perceptions can be created and exaggerated to make someone seem a lot better or worse than they are. This has been used successfully in political propaganda and PR work.

State of mind impacts perception

Emotional states such as fear, love, greed, anger, and delusion can cloud our perceptions. Often, what we perceive as a threat might not be a real threat at all. For instance, when a little spider is scurrying towards us, we may jump in fear. The spider, fearing for of its life, rushes to the nearest place for safety, which could end up being your foot – making you scream even louder. In reality, the spider is probably more scared than you are – and certainly not a threat!

Similarly, some parents, fearing the loss of love from their offspring, may perceive their in-law as a threat, thus creating marital conflict:

Amy appeared worried and restless on a long haul flight back to the Far East. Her delicate pretty face was racked with sadness. She had just run away from her husband and had no intention of returning. As much as she loved him, she could no longer cope with the daily bullying from her mother-in-law who lived next door. Her mother-in-law picked on everything she said and did: from housework to childcare; how Amy looked after her husband, and how she should peel a potato the Western way. All the harassment occurred behind her husband's back, driving a wedge between the young couple. Amy became more stressed and depressed, but her husband pleaded with her to put up with his mother for the sake of the family. Without much emotional support from people around her and with very few friends in England, Amy was lonely and struggling to be happy.

Amy expected her in-law to be kind and welcoming but her mother-in-law perceived Amy as a threat and so proceeded to treat her with contempt, eventually breaking up her son's marriage.

Expectation mars our vision. Students are reported to suffer from exam stress and the weight of parental expectations. Likewise, high expectations at work can result in some managers pursuing their big dreams without consulting their staff and a project ending in disaster.

Sue was appointed as a new manager in a large organisation. Eager to make her mark, she began to make substantial changes in the organisation. Sue expected the staff to cooperate with her new progressive plans. This brought a lot of resentment amongst the staff. Within a month, most of the staff were stressed out and began to protest, resulting in low productivity. Sue blamed them for being uncooperative and lazy. The staff perceived Sue as uncaring and having a significant lack of understanding of their needs and their company. Both sides wanted the company to succeed, but they couldn't and wouldn't compromise on the approach. It didn't help that Sue had not consulted her colleagues or other employees, and so she was left with more enemies and very little support. Within a year, Sue had to step down from her position and leave the company.

It is thus important to develop healthy perceptions right from the start.

Seeing things the way they are: perception of self

The biggest illusion we have is the perception of the self or of 'me, my, mine'. From a natural, realistic view, which part of 'my' body actually belongs to 'me'? If this body belongs to me, then I should have the authority to stop it growing taller or bigger, being sick, getting old and dying ... but that is not the case. This body goes through its natural cycle of constant change from when it comes into the womb and continues through childhood, adulthood, old age, and eventually death, when it then rots away. It belongs to nature, not to 'me' or a particular individual. The concept of 'me' and 'mine' has been learnt during childhood when we were given a name and introduced to other people in relation to ourselves. That is how we learn the concept of the self. And we hold on to it and build up the concept of self and ego(s). But if we look carefully, the brain that thinks this is 'me, myself, and my body' doesn't even belong to 'me'. The brain itself is made up of billions of cells. These cells communicate with each other via chemicals passing through the synapses. All of their communications occur independently of 'me'. Likewise, cells in other parts of the body communicate with each other in their own ways. When communication goes wrong, it results in illness, independent of 'my' control. When I die, nothing was actually 'me' nor remains 'me'. It is an illusion that we cling to and become stressed by trying to keep this 'me' satisfied.

The following situation illustrates how the perception of what is 'mine' can become ridiculous. You may recognise other similar scenarios:

On a crowded, long-haul flight, all the seats are occupied ex-

cept one between passengers A and B. Both A and B decide it is theirs. They eye each other to estimate their own chance of claiming the seat and thus maximise their own personal comfort. Passenger A starts putting his papers, pillow and blanket on the vacant seat while passenger B leans her elbow over the arm-rest and hauls her leg over to claim half the space. Neither wants to give up the seat for the other. Throughout the flight, any tiny invasion of space on that seat brings agitation and further attempts to take complete control – despite the fact that the seat belongs to neither person.

Give your perceptions a reality check. Try looking at situations from different perspectives before passing judgement – things are not always as they seem. Our perceptions may not always be right!

4 Balancing the mind

//

I wage war against my feelings,

John James Audubon

The mind is like a pendulum. In its neutral state, the mind is equanimous and at peace, ready to open up to new experiences without any bias. When the pendulum moves, our state of equilibrium is disrupted and shifts towards either side – towards a pleased or displeased feeling. The accompanying thoughts then align themselves with the 'like' or 'dislike' stance and are duly off-balance.

Differences between feelings and emotions

There are three types of feelings: liking, disliking, and indifference. We can also say that there are pleasant, unpleasant, and neither pleasant nor unpleasant feelings. The feeling of 'neither like nor dislike' does not mean a lack of interest. It means that the pendulum of your mind is not moved by the sense stimuli it comes into contact with; it is at peace. When an unpleasant feeling diminishes, a pleasant feeling arises – and vice versa. Inasmuch as we prefer pleasant feelings to unpleasant ones, leaning either way brings more restlessness. Out-of-balance feelings give rise to emotions. Emotion is a state of mind. Anger, fear, depression, frustration, and hopelessness are examples of states of mind.

Feelings and emotions change

The first experience of eating spicy hot chillies leaves you with a burning tongue. That burning sensation may last a few minutes or longer. Some time later you become accustomed to the taste, develop a fondness for it, and add more chillies to your food because you love the extra kick.

Working or living with someone you dislike for a long time can make or break you. You try to adjust and change your perception of them and start to like them or feel indifferent about them. Or you may develop an even stronger aversion to them.

Like the weather, emotions change swiftly from sunshine to hail, rain, and back to sunshine again in a short space of time. Passion fades, love dies. Nothing, except for the truth, lasts forever.

The brain, feelings, and emotions

Neuroscientists have found that the neurons in the amygdala – the fear and emotion centre – respond to visual, aural, and olfactory stimuli as well as to touch. If the amygdala finds sense stimuli threatening, it will press the alarm button. Stress hormones are released, the body is on stress alert, and emotional memory consolidation is enhanced. Painful events we want to forget are therefore saved in our memory bank. This may explain why traumatic memories can be triggered when PTSD (post-traumatic stress disorder) sufferers see/hear/smell/touch something that bears a small resemblance to the past.

We have a built-in spontaneous reaction, controlled by the amygdala, to any perceived threat. Seeing a child about to be hit by a fast moving car, we don't sit and think what to do. Our instinctive reaction is to grab the child and pull him or her to safety. This spontaneous mechanism helps to protect us from immediate danger. We react first and think later – when the information is sent to the analytical part of the brain.

Where do feelings come from?

Feelings can be aroused or activated by what we see, hear, smell, taste, and touch. The signals are sent to the brain for interpretation, and we respond to them accordingly. We may feel good or bad about them, depending on our associated thoughts and preconceptions. Mentioning the word 'coffee' will whet the appetite of coffee-lovers: they will be able to see it, smell its aroma, and recall the delicious taste of it. The same word can even bring back romantic memories of having coffee with that special someone. On the other hand, those who have developed a dislike of coffee may recall its bitter taste, how fast it made their heart beat, or the thumping head-ache and nausea they experienced after drinking it.

The effect of these sense stimuli on our feelings, perceptions, thoughts, and corresponding reactions is so swift and auto-matic that we hardly notice it. The following scenario illus-trates the point:

Walking along the street, you spot a mother shouting at her toddler, who falls off the pavement and lands on the road. The mother may have shouted due to fear for the child's safety, or possibly because she is tired, grumpy, and annoyed. Already you may not like what you see, and you feel sorry for the child and condemn the mother's behaviour. As you walk on, you hear the sound of a car approaching, with loud music blaring out. Your thoughts automatically switch from the mother and child to the noisy car and its driver. Depending on whether or not you like the music, your feet and fingers may start tapping along to the beat, or you might become irritated by the music and the inconsiderate driver. Only when the driver rolls down the window and shouts 'hello' do you discover that it's an old friend, and your irritation swiftly turns to pleasant surprise. As you continue walking to the high street, the pleasing aroma of freshly baked croissants from the local cafe hits you. Your thoughts shift to food. Such an aroma proves too tempting, and you like it: you walk into the cafe, only to find your ex sitting there with someone new. The sight automatically triggers resentment (and) recalling past negative memories. Your appetite vanishes as hurt and anger flood through you. You leave the cafe without the croissant but instead with strong feelings and thought seasonings that agitate you for hours.

Distorted perception of sense stimuli

The classical conditioning theory by Pavlov showed how repeatedly pairing the provision of food with the sound of a bell will make a dog salivate. Eventually salivation is triggered solely by the sound of the bell, without the presence of food. Another similar experiment conducted by Watson and Rayner involved Baby Albert, who was unafraid of a white rat. Only after a loud bang was paired repeatedly with the rat did Baby Albert develop a fear of rats. Both experiments showed how the perception of our sense stimuli can be distorted through conditioning, its effects on feelings of liking and disliking, and the emotions that followed. In a similar manner, those who have lived through wars may react with fear to sudden loud noises, as they are associating these sounds with past atrocities, even though the war finished long ago. It is therefore important to look into the impact of these sense stimuli on our feelings and the way in which the mind holds onto the past, causing us to suffer the emotional consequences.

The five sense stimuli

Sight

The impact of sight can be more than meets the eye. A study by Younger et al., for example, showed that looking at pictures of one's romantic partners stimulated the reward centres in the brain, helping to reduce pain. Disliking the sight of someone, a bully can provoke a violent fight. The sight of blood, a hairy spider, or a slithering snake can trigger a phobia in those who dislike such things, leading to an increase in cortisol release. Tranquil scenery, on the other hand, is pleasing to the eyes and therefore brings relaxation. Witnessing a fatal accident or a natural disaster is an unpleasant experience which can lead to trauma or a long-term impact on the memory.

Sound

Sound affects us physically, mentally, and emotionally. Hence its successful use in therapy! National anthems bring out people's patriotism. Music is used to set the scene in movies – stirring up pleasant and unpleasant feelings associated with love, fear, or suspense. You may find yourself tapping your fingers and feet to the uplifting rhythms, feeling mellow thanks to soothing soundscapes, driven to tears by heart-wrenching orchestral writing, or inspired by soaring melodies, depending on what you are listening to and whether or not it appeals to you.

Unfavourable noises can be frightening, agitating, deafening, and disturbing. An unpleasant voice can aggravate the listener. When left in a dark room on your own, a startling sound can easily make you jump. Even the slight sounds of a whisper can be upsetting if we tune into them and perceive the whispers as malicious gossip.

Taste

Eating food that is alien to your liking makes you feel awful.

Certain delicacies from around the world, such as raw meat, tadpoles, insects, snakes, rats etc. can be a real put-off for some but a delight for those who have more adventurous tastes. However, when given no other alternatives for food, some may develop a liking for them. Similarly, the first sip of alcohol may not be to one's liking, but, several social functions later, one begins to enjoy and drink more of it. Strong preferences and cravings for certain foods can easily lead to over-indulgence, addiction, obesity, and various health risks.

Smell

The strong pungent smells of some cheese, fermented foods, or smelly fruits are delightful for those who like them but can make others retch. The odour of freshly cooked food in market stalls stimulates the appetite and attracts customers. Some fragrances induce sexual stimulation or bring about a feeling of nostalgia. Olfactory stimuli have a strong impact on our memory and have been used in certain therapies to restore the memory of patients with head injuries and short-term memory loss.

Touch

Studies show that maternal touch is important for the survival of baby animals: a lack of maternal touch was found to contribute to behavioural and health problems in young children. Touching or indeed hugging helps to reduce stress levels, is crucial in a loving relationship, and helps to comfort those who are upset or frightened. Moreover, touching helps with oxytocin (a bonding hormone) release – without which some relationships can just fade away. However, being touched by someone you dislike can lead to a feeling of repulsion. Touching something soft, warm, smooth, and cuddly may bring a pleasing sensation, whereas rough, sharp, and cold objects may bring the opposite. Having to cut up a cold, slimy frog in a biology lesson can be stressful and leave one feeling squeamish. Feeling overheated or freezing cold can also cause stress, affecting one's concentration and sleep.

For any sense stimuli to make an impact, our mind has to take interest in them. If your mind takes no interest in them, they will be just passing sensations. Why would a faint noise from next-door bother you when the rest of your family has taken no notice of it? Why do you choose to be annoyed with one particular sound when there is a lot of background noise in the environment? Is it because you dislike that particular noise, or because it belongs to someone you dislike, or because it reminds you of an unpleasant experience from the past? When it is caught on your mind's radar, an alarm signal is raised, and you get agitated.

When we talk about sense stimuli, we can't discard those which arise and are felt and dwelled on by the mind. These arising thoughts and feelings are known as 'mind-objects'; they are unfiltered and can cloud the mind with either good or bad feelings. For example:

When listening to a song on the radio, our ears come into contact with the sound, and we hear the song; we like the sound and imagine a cool and attractive singer in our mind. As a result of liking the sound, the tune gets stuck in our head, we crave it, we memorise the words, and we find ourselves humming it on the bus, in the shower – everywhere. We become attached. The day we see this singer on TV, we realise that he looks nothing like what we had imagined and are hugely disappointed. But funnily enough, we may look for other likeable aspects (the way he walks, what he wears, his manner of speech) to make up for the visual input failing to satisfy so that we can carry on liking. We cling onto this 'liking', distorting the reality and building him up to become our idol. Our mind is clouded by this strong 'like', and we scream hysterically and feel faint in his presence. Or perhaps we may object to some bad language he uses on TV and stop liking him. This dislike leads to further bias, and we may stop buying his CDs completely in the future.

Dealing more effectively with sense stimuli

We may be programmed to act spontaneously to a threat in order to survive, but we can still train the mind to stay calm and respond with a positive manner when needed. When a sight comes into contact with your eyes, acknowledge it, mentally saying: 'seeing, seeing, seeing'. If you like or dislike it, it is 'feeling, feeling, feeling'. Try this with other sense stimuli.

One example would be when your teenager 'tests the boundaries'. If, in your head, you start complaining about how they have left dirty dishes piled up in the sink, it's just 'thinking, thinking, thinking'. If you dislike their trendy haircut, it's 'feeling, feeling, feeling'. If you look at their outburst/behaviour as a sight entering your eyes, the harsh words as sound entering your ears, and your anger as a mental object that arises in your mind, it doesn't seem so bad. It helps you to see things for what they really are, to remain neutral and not to take things too personally. You will be able to listen to their views and not feel the need to exercise your parental control. After all, neuro-scientists have discovered that our frontal brain (responsible for reasoning, making judgements) is not fully developed until we are in our early twenties. These youngsters are learning to become adults – with their hormones and their body developing at a fast speed.

Analyse things/situations from the perspective of the six senses, and stressful situations don't seem that bad. They are merely interactions between your sense organs and sense stimuli, which give rise to feelings of like and dislike, and further thoughts and emotions. You can then shift your mind's focus from an emotional reaction to reasoning instead.

Watch your feelings and emotions

Observe how feelings start, develop, and end. For example, when something happens, do I like it or not like it? Or do I feel indifferent to it? When liking arises in your mind, know that it has arisen; acknowledge it and see what happens next after you like something; are you aware of the liking disappearing? How does it disappear? Note down, step by step, what happens in your mind. Two scenarios are shown in the chart below.

Scenario 1: **An upsetting emotion**	Scenario 2: **A worry about meeting someone you don't like**
Disliking his tone of voice and manner	Disliking the prospect, not wanting to see her
Feeling irritated, annoyed and upset	Imagining what could go wrong at the meeting
Recalling past similar events when he upset you	Reviewing what went wrong in the past, getting more agitated
Fuming	Confirming that your fear was valid
Wanting to retaliate, challenge, or punish	Giving up
Isolating yourself, sulking	Calling off the meeting

Note down, step by step, and you can see what your mind (was) is doing. In the first scenario one holds on to the past, and in the second, one worries about the future.

Feelings are felt in the mind – the mind that mistakes this body, thoughts, feelings, and emotions as the self. It feels as if one is carrying a big burden on one's shoulder. The longer one carries, the heavier the burden. We know we need to offload. We put the burden down temporarily and we pick it up, putting it back on again because it feels familiar – a habit. We need to teach the mind to see what is it doing so it will understand and able to let go by itself.

Below is a diagram to remind you.

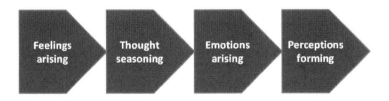

Emotions

If the mind is the sea, emotions are its movements. Sometimes it is calm. At other times it is stormy and angry and ...without any warning, a tsunami, destroying everything in its path.

When we experience any emotions, our state of mind is set in motion, moved, and stirred. Here we will look at some examples of the states of mind. Anger will be discussed in Chapter 5.

Anxiety

Anxiety makes things seem worse than they really are. An assignment may seem impossible, the housework insurmountable, the separation too frightening. We can also develop fear and anxiety through hearing repeated comments and stories:

Jo, a competent driver from a small town in the US, moved to London recently. Not knowing her way around, she felt nervous about taking a driving test. She mentioned it to her friends – most of whom told her about how many times they had failed their tests and how scary the examiners were. On the day of her test, she was met with a stern examiner. The words of her friends echoed in her ears, and she was less confident. Nervous, Jo began to make a few errors. She apologised to the examiner, who seemed completely unsympathetic. She was convinced that he didn't like her and that he was going to fail her, and she started making more mistakes. Sure enough, after the test, Jo joined the group of people who carried on telling their stories of their failed driving tests!

Repeated discouraging stories can play havoc on one's fears at critical moments if we let the mind bring them in without filtering them first. When we hear the same story repeatedly, we may start to believe it even when it's not true.

Sadness

When hope is gone, sadness arises. Loneliness, pain, and fear may begin to cave in from all sides. Stuck in such an emotional framework, one's perception narrows. When this happens, remind yourself that it's just emotion - a state of mind. It's not you. Be mindful of it. Like thorns, emotions can prick and pierce through your mind when you are not mindful of them. Do not season your thoughts or emotions. Ask yourself whether the arising emotion is positive or negative. If it's negative, then find something else to focus on. Break the chain of negative thoughts that fuels negative emotion and prompts negative action.

When Nelly and her husband went out as a couple, he criticised her clothes and belittled her. At party functions, she was usually left at the table all by herself while he joked with his friends and danced with others. Nelly's mother-in-law repeatedly told her that she was stupid and not good enough. Nelly felt trapped and unhappy and suffered a total loss of confidence. She became increasingly isolated, staying at home looking after her 2-year-old daughter.

Overwhelmed by depression and anger towards her husband and his family, Nelly slipped out of bed one night and decided to leave. She didn't even know where she was going. As she put her shoes on, she heard some noise from upstairs. Her daughter was crawling on her tummy down the stairs in the dark looking for her. Nelly hugged her daughter tight and burst into tears. Her hasty thought and action would have deprived her daughter of a mother. Nelly had come to her senses and finally learnt to assert herself, stood up against her husband and his family, and turned her life around!

It can take a few seconds for us to act on an emotion and that can cause tragedy or long term damage. Be aware and beware of such negative emotions.

On being happy

We all want to be happy. We want more of it. Happiness co-exists with unhappiness. They are the two sides of the same coin! To attain the happiness you crave, you need to work through misery and unhappiness. It's like eating a mango or a pineapple. The end next to the stem tastes sweeter than the other end which is slightly tangier. If we start eating from the sweet side, the fruit gets sourer towards the other end. If we start eating from the sour end, we will find that it gradually gets sweeter and sweeter. But some of us may give up half way through the sour bit before reaching the sweet success. Some may eat the sweet part and reserve the sour part for cooking. Likewise, in life, we can make the most of the sour bit or the stressful bit, or work through it to get to the sweet other side. The sour bit helps us appreciate the sweeter taste a lot more. We can also turn the sour bit into something new that will enhance its taste as well as our life!

Sometimes what we regard as happiness is just pleasure. Too much pleasure can be suffocating. Many of us may prefer a leisurely lifestyle to hard work, where we can just relax and have fun! It would be bliss – so you think! After a week of doing absolutely nothing, the bliss soon wears off. You'd soon be get bored stiff and have to start looking for new challenges. When pleasure subsides, dissatisfaction and unhappiness emerge naturally. There is no need to go and top up your happy mood. The emotion will change again. Once it dips down to its baseline, it will perk up, provided that you don't season it.

Can you trust your emotions?

When the mind is moved by emotion, it can't see or think clearly. Our perception is therefore distorted and our account of the upsetting incident may not be accurate. Once the emotion has settled, we may perceive the incident in a different light.

The more you look, observe, and understand feelings and emotions – pleasant and unpleasant – for what they truly are, the less chance feelings and emotions can move you, and the more your inner peace can be restored and strengthened.

5 Calming

the angry mind

//
When anger rises, think of the consequences,

Confucius

Some years ago, I was staying at a cosy, timbered, thatched farmhouse in the rolling hills of South Devon, when, at the crack of dawn, I was woken up by a loud, rude commotion. Looking out of the window, I saw a group of people surrounding a big tree and shouting abusive words at it. "It's anger management training for London executives", apologised my landlady over breakfast, "Apparently, it helps them get rid of their anger".

Can shouting in this way change one's angry habit? And as for that poor tree, how will it grow? Were they properly addressing the cause or the symptoms of their anger? What does shouting do to your body, muscles, and throat? In order to shout like that, you need to recall the infuriating incident and re-live it – to let out the anger. Will this erase the anger from your memory once and for all? How can you learn to manage your anger in the future? Shout at someone or at another tree? Looking for a scapegoat is an easy option, but what if the scapegoat happens to be your spouse, child, colleague, or employee, instead of a tree?

Our precious present moments are wasted when we are consumed by anger. It is buzzing in our ears, occupying our head, clouding our mind, and zapping our energy. Angry behaviour is associated with a higher risk of heart disease and stroke – all the more reason why you need to consider carefully the impact of your anger. Learn to assert yourself in a calmer manner and channel it in the right direction. Consider also what one looks like in such a state. Blood rushes to our face, turning it red.

Adrenaline is released and facial muscles are tightened. The hair stands up, pupils enlarge; body temperature rises, and our body produces sweat to cool itself down. Now we look and smell bad.

Powered by one's own thought seasonings, some people enjoy a splurge of their anger; they are able to speak their mind without holding back but may regret their outburst afterwards. It is like overeating indigestible food that has been made especially to one's own palate. You feel bloated, unable to breathe, and wish you hadn't indulged so much.

The anger chain reaction

Left unmanaged, anger spreads fast like weeds, occupying the whole garden and destroying good plants in its path. When feeling irritated, you might confront your spouse, child, or even a total stranger in the street. Maybe it's something they have said or perhaps it's their body language that makes you snap. Annoyed and confused by your bad mood, these people may then take out their negative feelings on their friends or someone else. Your bad temper could cause your spouse to lose concentration while driving or be the reason why your children go off to school feeling upset and unconfident, unable to focus on their studies. Regular angry outbursts can have a damaging effect on one's children. Scientists have found that children do not have fully developed prefrontal brains to help deal with emotions, and they can be prone to depression.

Bottle up anger, and we may explode. But suppressing it can lead to depression. Brush it aside and there it will remain - rotting away and intoxicating your mind. By rejecting your anger, you give it significance, and so are unlikely to forget it. We may seek other outlets – dial a friend or post the issue on social media. This anger soon spreads around like a virus, leading to more casualties. Those who are on the receiving end and those who side with us can also suffer in various ways.

Make a business call or send an email while you are feeling irritable, and you may lose a client or upset a relationship. One person's bad mood can even set off a global chain reaction of irritability and anger at the touch of a keyboard button, spreading within minutes. Anger is infectious! Others will pick up on your mood and pass it on. Long-term anger towards neighbours, colleagues, or whoever can turn into revenge, dragging family members and other people into a hate war: once you have got an enemy, you need some allies to protect yourself. You might tell your close friends about your 'horrible' neighbour. Siding with you, your friends may dislike your neighbour without even getting to know them. And your neighbour might do the same. Friends on both sides may develop a dislike of each other even though they have never met, starting a negative chain reaction.

From winner to angry monster

Some surveys suggest that fear of death comes second to fear of public speaking. However, an enraged person has no fear. When angry, one can quickly become very vocal together with strong eye-contact and intense body language. The grumpy monster within can sometimes turn us into a bully who wants to bring down others' joyous moods. 'What right have they got to be so happy when I'm not?' We are ready to argue. Winning an argument makes us feel good, and our ego expands. The bigger it gets, the more pampering it needs, leaving us prone to fits of anger should we not get our own way. However, allowing anger to get the upper hand demonstrates how weakness of mind can be fuelled by negative thinking. The true winner is the person who conquers his own mind and remains unshaken regardless. Such calm comes directly from within. When your mind is in the right place, the right thoughts and actions will follow.

How to deal with anger

'I just flipped', 'I didn't know what I was saying', 'I was over-come by rage at the time, and I felt so bad afterwards'. Such responses are understandable; however, in difficult circum-stances when both parties are upset, the best strategy is to keep silent.

Anger is like a child who doesn't get what he or she wants. The child may throw tantrums, get upset, boycott their food, and be unable to enjoy anything else until the parents give in or give them love and attention. If the parents give in, the child's anger is nurtured and can get worse as the years go by. What an angry child needs is love and attention. Similarly, you need to give your anger the attention it needs by listening to it, being patient with it, and observing and understanding it. The anger will naturally calm down, just as will a child's. Be with your anger and be mindful of it (see Chapter 7) without passing judgement. Developing loving kindness (see Chapter 8) will help you become more patient with your anger. You need not only to listen to your anger but also to educate your mind in order to see the risks and damage to yourself and others when it clings to anger. Here are some suggestions:

To be angry is to harm oneself

To hurt others, you have to think of strong words to inflict pain. While you are thinking of the words, your mind is in turmoil. Physically, your heart is working faster, your internal organs are under pressure from stress, your blood is pumping faster, your facial muscles are twisted, and your body is tensed and aching. You have already tortured yourself to come up with hurtful words. When those words are spat out with furious force and volume, your throat hurts, too. You may gain momentary satisfaction at the price of your own physical and mental health risks. If the other person is not in the least bit affected by your harsh words, you will be left fuming even more. That person may be unpleasant, but you don't need to act in the same way.

Have a glass of water. Your internal organs are working hard, burning up lots of energy to fuel your anger. Your body and skin may be dehydrated. An anger habit can lead to early signs of ageing, such as wrinkles, and may speed up the process as well. If you want good-looking skin, keep that anger under control!

Sleeping on your anger and it can give you nightmares, causing you to swear, hit, and punch the air in your sleep. Your partner may suffer sleep loss and become irritable the next day. Now you've got two grumpy people in the house instead of one!

Anger gains two enemies: within and without

The anger that you have directed at a total stranger may come back to haunt you. You will never know whether that stranger might become a future manager or colleague who could put in a bad word and cost you your job. You have so much to lose when you let your anger get the better of you.

It's much better to turn enemies into allies. This will contribute to a more harmonious working environment, and you may gain some support from these former enemies in the workplace or in the community. Social support is essential in reducing stress.

Congratulations if you manage to keep silent while fuming with anger. You have avoided creating an outside enemy. If, however, you still carry that anger around in your mind, then you are creating an enemy within. This inside enemy is far more dangerous, because we are oblivious to its power of destruction.

This inside enemy can haunt us and bring about fear. We may fear the possible rumours that the enemy out there will be spreading to tarnish our reputation, feel a need to be on guard, and then be unable to relax. Deal with the inside enemy straight away by being mindful of your thoughts to prevent further negative thinking.

Your anger can hurt the person you love

Avoid using your family as an outlet for your anger. They are there to help you, support you, and be on your side. Being angry at them when it's not their fault can create a lot of hurt and pain and lead to them turning against you. Bullying or using violence means that you may need help before things get much worse. Losing support from your own family will bring intense emotional conflicts because you are in close daily contact with them, leaving you with nowhere to turn.

When you are angry, your views become narrower and focus mainly on the negatives. Try to look at others' good points. Make a list of the nice, positive things they have done as a reminder of their good nature. Nobody is perfect. We are not perfect either – otherwise, we wouldn't get ourselves stuck in this negative state for so long and so often! Furthermore, if you keep losing your temper, be aware that you may set a negative example for your children. Your children may learn to respond negatively to stress in exactly the same way you've shown them.

Free yourself from past anger

Recalling an angry situation is enough to quicken your breathing and your heartbeat. What is the point in re-living your anger and kick-starting your stress response? Whatever happened in the past has ended. There is no point in reviving it and imprisoning yourself with that pain over and over again. Bullies will suffer their own physical and mental health risks due to their negative thoughts and actions. Past anger, fuelled and set alight by our thought seasoning process, burns us from within, destroying the kindness in our heart and our sense of right and wrong. Harmful action may follow.

Anger can be expensive

If you are one of those who expresses your anger aggressively by slamming the door or hurling things at someone, then you may find that you are left to pick up the cost of the damage. Why create extra work for yourself? Angry wives may blow their bank balance in one shopping spree or worse, file for an expensive divorce. In addition to damage and destruction, the cost of treating ill health due to accumulated anger and stress can be very expensive as well.

Make those angry memories redundant

The brain is very selective in storing memories and discarding what we don't need. Adding emotions and thought seasonings to any incident makes the brain more likely to store the memory, and you may remember it for a long time afterwards. Therefore, it is best to know that your angry emotions will pass sooner or later: see them as passing sensations and nothing else.

Give your mind something else to focus on

When angry, your stress response provides you with extra energy. Make better use of it. Instead of spending a day or two mulling over the past, why not do something for the benefit of yourself and others? Spend your extra energy doing exercise and improving your brain function, or try doing some cleaning round the house, giving you a more pleasant environment, which can uplift your mood. You will achieve something worthwhile. Be at one with the activity at hand. Get rid of your anger whilst chopping off dead branches, pruning, watering the plants, sweeping up dead leaves, cutting the grass. You will get a beautiful garden that provides peace and calm. Your mood will soon change. Or you can attune your senses to your natural surroundings and preoccupy yourself with relaxing activities.

Identify the stimuli that trigger your anger

Make a list of what tends to drive you berserk and what senses trigger your negative reaction. Look at the pattern of your own reactions:

•   Does noise aggravate you? What type of noise irritates you most? (lawn mowers, telephones, hoovering, screaming babies, loud music/TV from next door, swear words) Be aware that your hearing sense is disturbed. How much does it bother you? How do you react to auditory disturbance?

•   Do people's words tend to upset you? Or is it their manner of speaking? What senses have been affected: hearing, sight, or thoughts towards these people?

•   Is it a smell that irritates you? Why? How much does it bother you? Does the smell bring back some unpleasant memories?

• Do other people do things which upset you? How? Are they being too fast, too slow, too rude, or too rigid? Or does their behaviour trigger painful memories from the past? Which senses do they trigger?

• Do you get angry when things don't go your own way? (your computer always breaks down, the traffic is too slow, people are interfering with what you want to do, etc.) What senses have been stirred? Is it sight, hearing, touch, smell, taste, mental objects (past memories), or all of these?

Notice some patterns in your reactions and behaviour. Do the things that irritate you have a similar effect on others? Why or why not? If they have no impact on others, then why are they having an impact on you? Is it because you are in the mindset that you can't tolerate these things, allowing them to continue annoying you? Before reacting, ask yourself what sense is being affected and why. This will delay your emotional response and eventually will lead to you reacting less to irritating sense stimuli. How would you rate yourself on a 'tolerance' scale from 0–10 when any of these stimuli, which you've deemed unfavourable, occur (with 0 being intolerant and 10 being highly tolerant)? If your tolerance score towards someone is zero, ask yourself whether it's the sight, sound, smell, or the way he/she behaves. Identify these sense stimuli and note them down so you can understand the process of your anger and deal with it more effectively.

An angry person is stupid, an outraged person insane

I asked one of my meditation teachers why it was so difficult to get rid of anger. She replied, 'Getting rid of anger isn't difficult. Just remember: An angry person is stupid; an outraged person is insane. (When you are angry, you say and do a lot of stupid things that you will regret afterwards. And when you are in rage, you behave like a mad person.) Which one do you want to be, stupid or insane?' she asked. 'Neither,' I replied. 'In that case,' she said, 'just stop being angry!' When we are angry, we are no smarter than an idiot.

Develop empathy for others

Life is not what it seems. Never assume that others are happier than you, and use them as a scapegoat of your anger. We need to take responsibility not to put others in despair with our unkind words and actions just because we are in a foul mood. If you are on the receiving end of the anger, don't take it personally. Keep in mind that the angry person might be under a lot of pressure. If you respond to anger with calmness, it will help to calm the angry actions or reactions of others.

Smile!

We may not be aware of our own grumpy facial expression, but people tend react to it. Just imagine… you wake up in the morning feeling a bit tired. You don't feel like doing anything, but you need to go to work. You enter the dining room with a frown. Your partner and children take one look at you and think: what have we done to deserve such a face? They might choose to ignore you, or they might take it personally. Be aware of the face you put out there. Add a smile whenever you can. You don't need an excuse to smile. Give yourself at least ten smiles before you get out of bed. Endorphins will be released in your brain, making you happy and enabling you to begin the day in a good mood. Endorphins can also numb your physical pain. So if you are in pain, smile!

When young children get upset, you can try this simple technique to get them out of their moods. Ask them whether they are happy feeling the way they feel. They will say no. You can then ask whether they want to be happy. They'll probably nod or say yes. Then you can ask them to give you a big smile. It may sound silly but it works. Tell them to give you a really big smile like a Cheshire Cat – a big grin from ear to ear. They may show some resistance or just give a little smile at the corners of their mouths. You can then ask them to make the smile wider and wider each time. In no time at all, they will start giggling and forget about their feeling upset.

The same works for adults. In a state of anger, try smiling. The angrier you are, the wider your smile needs to be. You can't remain angry for long!

Look at your anger

Take a short sharp breath and then breathe out your anger. Make it fast. Do this a couple of times. When you breathe out, send the grumpy mood out with your breath. Now look at your anger. See what it's like. Does it have a temperature, colour, or any sensations attached to it? Watch it and see how long it lasts before other thoughts start arising.

Some may wonder how on earth you can look at your anger when all you can see is the person, thing or situation that is upsetting you. Indeed! When you look outward with your eyes, you see this 'annoying' thing. When you are angry, this thing in front of you seems to be the worst possible kind. This is because you look with your eyes and then season your thoughts with past memories and feelings. This fires up your anger even more.

To see your anger, you need to look within. Close your eyes and look inwards. You may notice the sound of your heart pounding fast and heated emotions bubbling inside. Maybe you see colours, red or black, or a burning fire. You might feel as though there is something stuck in your throat. Some may feel nauseated. Look at your anger and be with it while it lasts. You will see that it soon disappears of its own accord as long as you don't add further thoughts to it. It came and went, just like that. That is all there is to it, unless we choose to pick up on it again. But why would we?

Learn to forgive

To counter a vengeful anger, one needs to do something completely opposite: that is to show kindness and forgiveness. Studies show that forgiving reduces your heart rate, blood pressure, and stress levels. It also improves your mental and physical health. Holding grudges prolongs stress, damaging your peace of mind and ruining your health. Whatever happened in the past belongs to the past and is no longer relevant now. Don't let anger ruin the joy you can have right now. Forgive, let go, and restore your peace of mind.

There's a difference between thinking of forgiving and actually forgiving someone. You need to take action to forgive. You may want to write several letters to the person (without necessarily sending them) saying that you have forgiven them. Or visualise this person in front of you and say to this person that they are forgiven. Do this several times a day. Or you may choose to send loving kindness to this person. Visualise this person in front of you and mentally say 'May you be happy!' Do this every day until you really mean it and are able to say it with ease.

Respond with positive action

Do something positive and different from what you normally

do when you are angry. If you tend to insist that things must go your way, from now on, let others have things their way in order to disintegrate your angry habit. Tell yourself: I'm not nurturing this angry monster, and I'm not going to let it get the best of me! If you tend to sulk, you may try singing instead. Or even better, try being especially nice to your rival! Don't let your anger have the upper hand – you no longer have to be a slave to your anger.

Julie used to have problems with some bossy women in her social group. Every time she saw them, she got irritated. Often she walked away to avoid further conflict. This didn't improve the situation, so she decided to do something against her inner contempt. Every day she forced herself to greet them with a smile and kind words. It was very hard at first. But the more annoyed she was, the wider her smile and the kinder her words. Her efforts eventually paid off. Those women were surprised by her change of tone. Her positive change of character made these women change the ways they communicated with her. They became nicer and kinder to her. Julie discovered later that they all had a lot in common and that they were not as bad as she had perceived them to be. New friendships were established, and they now enjoy each other's company. Julie was glad that she hadn't nurtured her irritation and isolated herself.

With continuous practise, you will have more control over your actions. Your new optimistic behaviour will be infectious, creating a new chain of positive reaction that reaches out and touches others in a more harmonious way.

Lower our expectations

We all have expectations. It's hard enough living up to our own expectations but we expect that of others as well. Hence we have more to feel unhappy and irritated about - from the poor performance of our children, spouse, employees, to that of our colleagues and more. If we lower our expectations and look at their other potentials or qualities, we won't feel too upset about their inadequacies. Note down their positive traits. Every time we get angry, we can have a look at this list to remind ourselves that nobody is perfect - including ourselves.

Our expectations can prolong the existing anger. If, for example, we expect an apology and it doesn't come soon enough, we can't enjoy the present moment. Our expectation clouds the mind, enslaving it, locking us in the past and keeping us waiting….to be happy. Why not free ourselves from such ridiculous expectations and enjoy the present moment now?

Write things down

According to studies, writing about your feelings has a therapeutic effect and increases your immunity; it helps to release your frustration and anger. Express your anger, pain and agony on paper. Be creative, using metaphor and simile. Put the paper away for a few days. When your anger has subsided, rip up the paper and toss it away.

Sooner or later we will all pass away

Extreme anger can come with dark vengeful thoughts: the mind becomes muddy and murky as we plot revenge. But what's the point of hurting or harming others when we will all eventually pass away naturally anyway? If we keep nourishing such negative thoughts, we will be the ones who put ourselves in serious health risk first. If you are angry with your beloved, the negative feelings that arise can be quite intense. This is because the opposite of love is hate. When love diminishes, the contrast of love becomes more evident. Life is too short. Don't waste your time and energy getting angry. Before lashing out with those unkind words, remind yourself that you don't want to regret this unkind action when they pass away.

What exactly are you angry with?

When others say something hurtful, where exactly on your body does it hurt? Your head, your arm, neck, legs? None! Most people say it hurts their heart. This shows that hurt does not occur on the body but inside. Your heart may be pumping much faster because of anger, and if you already have an existing symptom of heart disease, then you may experience some pain. But the heart does not carry this pain to the next hour or the next day. The mind does. If the pain is not on the body, then it must be in the mind.

Our body and that of the other person we are angry with belong to nature – just like a tree. We don't get angry with an odd-shaped tree. If the tree gets diseased, we treat and trim it. If we look at a person like that, we don't get angry with their body, do we? So are we angry with their mind? What does their mind look like? Does it have any shape or form? None! So what are we really angry at?

Go ahead, get angry, but don't stop!

If you have tried everything and your mind still dwells on anger, let it carry on fuming. BUT, for the maximum pleasure of getting angry, tell the mind that it is not allowed to stop. It must be angry all day and night. And you will keep watch on it.

You'll notice how ridiculous getting angry is. If you tell yourself to continue getting angry without stopping, you will lose the desire to be angry.

Notice, too, how your thought seasonings keep the anger alive – how anger boils up, erupts, burns out and then cools down. No need to brush away your thoughts. Watch and be mindful of those thoughts – you can learn a great deal from them. It's okay to feel angry as long as you don't harm anyone – including yourself. When you keep watching the mind, it stops misbehaving.

Contemplate the identity of self

We identify ourselves as a providing husband, a dutiful wife, a caring mum, a maturing teen, a clever and capable person … we have a rigid sense of self, of who we are and what we should be. This sense of self can be over-inflated. The greater our ego, the more likely we are to get frustrated and irritable with the incompetence of others. Try the following exercise when you are angry:

Sit comfortably and allow your eyes to close gently. Now look at yourself, sitting there with this burning anger. Then look deeper inside at your anger without adding any judgement. Simply look at it.

You'll notice that there is

• 	a breathing body

• 	an angry emotion

• 	a consciousness that is looking at both the body and the anger

All three are separate identities.

The body is like a puppet, pulled into action by enraged thoughts when the mind moves into an angry state. The mind dictates the body and orders it to deliver aggression and harsh speech. The mind holds on to hurt, absorbs the pain, and holds onto an emotional scar and painful memories. This pain lies dormant, waiting to be triggered. Any time the anger is triggered, the pain breaks loose. Anger rises as a result of your own interpretation of a situation. The mind can make mountains out of molehills: one can get angry about absolute nonsense. A minor incident can be blown out of proportion, triggering the stress response into action. This physical body that we call 'self' does not get angry. Our mind does. It is unhappy because it darts here and there aimlessly without guidance, collecting emotional garbage, then getting lost in it.

Next time you find yourself wanting to shout at trees, try some of the above techniques and see which ones work better for you.

6 Accepting change and uncertainty

Change is happening all the time; sometimes it's barely noticeable. As a child, we want to grow up fast. This makes the gradual physical changes seem like forever. Once we become adults, we want the changes to stop, but our cells keep on changing, allowing us to age.

We make minute changes all day without being conscious of them. For instance, being on your feet for too long is tiring; you need to sit down. After a while, you have to adjust your posture by leaning to the right or the left or by crossing your legs. We welcome change as long as it pleases us. When change, such as losing one's job or the sudden death of loved one, threatens our emotional security, change becomes unbearable. Our negative attitude towards change and uncertainty, in itself, make us unhappy, especially when it is not in line with nature.

All living things change and move towards decay – be they a tree, animal, or a person. As we grow older, the production of beneficial hormones such as the DHEA hormone, melatonin, testosterone, and oestrogen are naturally in decline. This allows us to age, unveiling all common characteristics of age. Being unaware of these changes, the mind takes it for granted that this body will last till old age and that it will withstand the abuse of an unhealthy lifestyle. At the same time, it grasps onto sensual pleasure, love, and relationships and wants them to last.

If we look closely at love and relationships, from when we fall in love till death do us part, we will see that some unavoidable changes come from nature itself. These natural changes impact the way we behave and feel towards each other. Understanding this will help us develop a healthier attitude towards change. At the same time, the mind will be taught to see things as the way they are. The examples given here do not in any way represent all relationships or go into all the complexities which can come with a relationship. These are just a few aspects of natural change that we are likely to come across.

One of life's natural processes is to procreate. Love, sex, and reproduction! Or sometimes just the latter two! Throughout the history of mankind, people have searched, suffered, and even died for love. Countless books, fiction and non-fiction, as well as poetry and songs have been dedicated to the topic of love alone. Love is romanticised as an elixir of life. Hence people continue to search for it on holiday, on the Internet, on blind dates, and at social gatherings – hoping to fill this void in their lives. Falling in love triggers the release of the stress hormone (cortisol) and other hormonal releases, affecting the feelings and behaviour of those in love. However, these high level hormonal releases can't continue forever. Even cortisol has a negative feedback system so that it can return to its baseline; otherwise, we would suffer ill health. As a result of natural hormonal readjustments, the intensity of emotion and passion do wane. With couples having other circumstances in their lives to deal with as well as having different ways of dealing with stress, any loving couple will have to adjust to changes throughout the course of love.

The nature of love and associated hormones

A study by Marazziti and Canale suggested that newly-in-love people had a higher cortisol level in their bloodstream than those who were not. The same research also found that men in love had lower testosterone release, whereas women had higher testosterone release. This may explain why men become gentler, more tamed, and more agreeable in order to win over their love, whilst women become more willing to take risks. Other studies have reported that the hormonal changes during ovulation and women's reproductive instinct impact their feelings and behaviour, making them more attractive to men. It is truly fascinating how love prompts chemical releases and changes in our personality, without us being conscious of it.

Uncertainty

What goes up must come down: likewise with hormonal release. According to neuroscientists, the intense feelings of love, passion, desire, euphoria, pleasure, trust, and sexual arousal are powered by hormones – chemical substances such as dopamine, serotonin, oxytocin, and vasopressin. They keep us addicted to love. Unfortunately, these hormonal releases were found to last only for a year or two. Once the honeymoon period is over, you may be left with a warm, cosy feeling – or perhaps boredom settles in, with a desire to move on.

If you ever wonder why your partner has changed and is no longer as attentive, caring, and passionate as he or she once was, now you know: it's partly hormones! So who is actually in love? Does love have anything to do with two individuals, you may wonder? Is this love for real if changing hormones can affect its longevity? Not understanding nature, this uncertainty can fuel hurt and pain.

And the changes keep on rolling …

Passion wanes, circumstances change. Disagreements are inevitable. The gender differences in dealing with stress add to more complexity in relationships.

Susan had a bad day and needed to get things off her chest. Like many women who like to talk to someone when they are stressed, she told her husband about it. Trying to comfort her, he assured her that her problems were no big deal and weren't worth getting uptight about. Susan was even more upset. She felt that he was being insensitive to her problem. She sulked. As far as her husband was concerned, when compared to all the stress at work he had to deal with, her problem was too trivial to waste time thinking about.

Generally speaking, when a woman talks about her problems, she just needs someone to listen – advice is not needed unless she asks for it. As men have a different approach to tackling problems, they may not appreciate this talking strategy and often try to suggest a solution, annoying the woman even more. Why not relieve her stress by giving her a few hugs instead? A study led by Dr Karen Grewen confirmed that hugging helps release oxytocin (a love/bonding hormone), reducing cortisol, blood pressure, and the risk of heart disease. Meanwhile, women should understand that the way that men respond is a result of the way the male brain operates, and they shouldn't take it personally – he is just trying to help in the way he knows best. Our mind expects certain reaction from loved ones. When we don't get it, we get upset. Our expectation is one thing. The gender differences in the way in which men and women use their brain and deal with stress are another.

Not only do men have a different way of dealing with stress than women, but an fMRI study led by Wang et al. showed that they use different parts of the brain when combating mental stress. The study showed an increase in blood flow in the right prefrontal cortex (associated with the fight or flight response) for men and an activation of the limbic (emotional) region for women. Men seem to use reason and confrontation in these situations, whereas women resort to their emotions. Women's limbic system has actually been found to be bigger than a man's. This could account for women's extra sensitivity. Other studies suggest that cortisol facilitates emotional memory in the amygdala, the emotion or fear centre in the brain. This may explain why when many women are stressed, all of a sudden their past memories come flooding back and all hell breaks loose – their emotional memories and emotional centre are activated. When things fall apart, more men than women were reported to turn to alcohol and harmful drugs to help them cope, and some even resort to suicide, with the numbers of men committing suicide around the world surpassing those of women. However, women are reported to be more at risk for depression than men.

Life has many uncertainties. Not many couples make it to their silver wedding anniversary. According to the UK's Office of National Statistics in 2010, one in three marriages end before their 15th anniversary and the average marriage now lasts 11.4 years.

To maintain a loving relationship, studies advise physical contact to stimulate the secretion of the bonding hormones oxytocin and vasopressin. Otherwise, kind words go a long way – watch what you say. Most importantly, keep in mind that all things are subject to change.

Further hormonal decline and mid-life crisis

From the age of 40 onwards, the production of sex hormones starts to decline, both in men and women. With less testosterone being released, some men put on weight and suffer from insomnia, fatigue, irritability, loss of sexual desire, and sexual impotency, and their thought process becomes slower. These symptoms are known as andropause, or the male menopause. Meanwhile, women's oestrogen levels also decline, thus offsetting a rise in cortisol production, which affects moods, irritability, and memory. Some women may also suffer from menopausal symptoms including hot flashes, night sweats, grumpy moods, loss of libido, sleeping problems, weight gain and mild cognitive dysfunction. Stress and excessive smoking and drinking are found to accelerate the menopause process in both men and women.

 The changes in sex hormonal release in middle age are found to have a negative impact on sleep for both sexes. With less sleep, cortisol levels increase, therefore starting a vicious cycle of sleeping difficulties and irritability. Understandably, those with severe symptoms may experience irritation and emotional outbursts due to their lack of sleep and exhaustion. If the increased levels of cortisol and sleep loss continue for a lengthy period of time, they can contribute to depression. Some studies found that women with a history of depression are at risk of relapse during the menopause. A decline in melatonin and serotonin production can further exacerbate sleep difficulties and mood problems.

The decline of sex hormones and DHEA (responsible for the protection of the hippocampus) also has a negative impact on memory for men and women. A number of menopausal women complain about being at a loss for words, being unable to complete sentences, and forgetting people's names. One theory blames this verbal memory deficit on menopausal hot flashes, which cause blood to rush to the face, depriving the brain of its usual blood flow. Another theory suggests that menopausal depression could account for memory problems. Sleeping difficulties from severe menopausal hot flashes and night sweats can also worsen memory problems. Debate is still ongoing over whether or not this verbal memory impairment is affected by menopause, stress, the ageing process, or sleeping problems and why not all menopausal women suffer this problem. Interestingly, some women suffer post-natal verbal memory deficiency as well. Whether this is due to fluctuating hormones or fatigue remains to be seen. By the time we have reached a ripe old age, our brains shrink in size naturally, meaning our memory can get even worse.

Can you imagine two middle age grumps living together, each suffering from insomnia, a low sex drive, and unable to find the words to communicate with each other? But don't panic – not everybody experiences the same menopausal symptoms, and the degrees of severity also vary. You might not be one of them! An understanding of these natural changes helps reduce our expectations and unreasonable demands on ourselves and others.

Otherwise we may have to resort to 'rent a family' – just like what they have in Japan. If you're not getting along with your own family or you haven't got a family of your own, you can adopt one. You can rent a family – grandparents, wife, and children – for a day out. Such a service comes at a hefty price but with no strings attached.

Embracing change

If you don't like the changes that take place, try changing your outlook, and everything else might start to change. If you don't like what you study, it's unlikely that you will do well in that subject. Why not find something you like about it so you can enjoy it more and do better? If you dislike how your partner stacks the dishwasher, why get annoyed every time you open it? You don't get anything out of it except bad mood. Why not change your attitude so you can be happier?

Embracing change frees your mind from agitation and restlessness. It also frees us from identity problems – that of being a wife, a husband, a mother, a father, a friend. Those labels come with certain forms of expectations that we have of them, and they of us. The safeguarding of our constructed identity can get out of hand, making ourselves and others unhappy. An empty nest prospect, for example, can be so daunting for some parents that they prefer the child to attend a university closer to home. The identity crisis is an illusion, created by expectations of how we and those related to us are supposed to be or act.

Change and uncertainty are with us every step of the way. Love and relationships are no exception. Understanding is the key to accepting, embracing, and coping successfully with them. It helps if we contemplate the nature of things often so that the mind will not cling onto people, situations, the past, and the future. We will come to accept things as they are and thus let go of unnecessary worries.

7 Training for
a mindful mind

With the mention of the word 'meditation', most people will immediately conjure up an image of someone sitting cross-legged in a tranquil environment, perhaps saying 'ohm'. Such an image is not wholly correct. Meditation is not restricted to a sitting position. Mindfulness meditation, for example, can be practised while sitting, standing, walking, or lying down; it can be done anytime and anywhere.

Mindfulness meditation

There are two ways to become mindful. One is to establish mindfulness, based on the four foundations: body, feelings, mind, and mind-object – to bring the mind to the present moment, to what we are doing, feeling, thinking, etc. The other is to develop wisdom in order to see clearly into the nature of things as they are – that all conditioned things are impermanent, and not self. These seeing and understanding need to come from insight rather than cognitive thinking. This insight allows the mind to let go of stress and attachments. Most teachings of mindfulness meditation outside the monastery tend to exclude this development of insight. This ancient Buddhist meditation training is non-religious and practical for all. Hence it has been adapted for many therapeutic uses.

Do not confuse mindfulness with visualisation techniques where you imagine being out there in a tranquil, relaxing environment – this is an altogether separate practice. When you are mindful, you focus within to see what's going on in your body and mind at that moment.

In the East, the ultimate aim of meditation practice is freedom from all suffering. In the West, the aim is geared towards health benefits. To date, studies on mindfulness meditation show numerous beneficial effects, from reducing stress, insomnia, anxiety, chronic pain, depression, aggression, weight, and eating and skin disorders to helping with trauma, sadness, and fear – to name but a few.

If you want a well-toned body, you need to take regular exercise and eat a healthy diet. As soon as you start to slack, the evidence on your waist, belly, and chin speaks for itself. Mindfulness requires regular practice. If you want to remain calm in the midst of stressful events, you need to work on your mind. There are many mindfulness techniques, and we will focus on some of them here.

Mindful breathing

Our state of mind and the breathing patterns are interrelated. When we are relaxed and resting, breathing becomes more comfortable, deeper, and longer. Short breaths are associated with stress and higher oxygen consumption, and they make the internal organs work harder in order to produce more energy. Alternatively, in a meditative state, the breathing becomes slower, steady, and so subtle that it seems as if you are not breathing at all. Studies show that during meditation, breathing rates and oxygen consumption drop, thus leading to less energy consumption and lower stress levels!

We can reduce our stress by changing our breathing pattern as follows:

Breathe deeply and slowly. Be aware of the sensation as the air enters your nostrils and fills up your lungs and down to your abdomen. When you breathe out, make it as long as possible, be mindful of the sensation, and let go of any worries or anxiety. Notice how your lungs and abdomen expand when you breathe in and contract again when you breathe out. Repeat this about 10 times and resume your normal breathing. Do not continue with deep breathing for too long, because you may experience discomfort and feel tired. Do just enough to change your shallow breathing pattern as needed.

Deep breathing is wonderful if you have too much chatter in your head and can't sleep. The secret to good sleep is to breathe out as long as possible. Do this as many times as you can, especially while lying in bed. Your thoughts will soon subside. Not only will you fall asleep faster but you will also get a better night's sleep.

One of my meditation teachers said that we only think whilst we breathe in, but we can't think properly whilst breathing out, especially when the out-breath is longer than the in-breath. Thought only arises when there is a tiny pause in your long out-breath. Dr James Austin, a renowned professor of neurology at the University of Colorado Health Sciences Centre, had similar findings. In his research on Zen meditation, Dr Austin observed that breathing-in seems to stimulate brain activity, whereas breathing-out did just the opposite. Hence, by making the out-breaths much longer than the in-breaths, you effectively reduce the brain's activity. Deprived of thoughts, the mind has nothing to dwell on, thus allowing you to naturally fall to sleep.

If you practise mindful breathing whilst sitting down, you need to get into a comfortable position. Make sure that your lower back is upright and that you are relaxed and comfortable. Don't sit leaning on the wall or the sofa; you'll get too comfortable and it is likely that you may nod off.

-       First, breathe in and be aware of your body. Breathe out and be aware of your body. Be aware of your body at all times as you breathe in and out. (As mentioned, you can do this while standing, sitting, walking, or lying down.)

-       Get to know your breath. Follow your breath in and out for a while. Notice whether they are long or short breaths. Are they coarse, heavy, light, or subtle? Is your inhalation longer or shorter than your exhalation? Observe and be mindful with every breath. Is your breathing relaxing and comfortable? Adjust your breathing accordingly.

-      Now that your breathing has become more comfortable and your body is relaxed and upright, focus your attention at the tip of your nose. As you breathe in and out, be aware of the sensation that the air touches the tip of your nose, but don't follow the breath. (You can do this while lying down, sitting, walking, or standing as well.) This is to establish calm and focus.

-      Feeling a bit calmer, you can shift the focus of attention to your abdomen. When you breathe in, the abdomen expands; that's the 'rising' sensation. When you are aware of this rising sensation, mentally say to yourself 'rising'. Breathing out, the abdomen contracts and deflates. When you are aware of the abdomen's deflating sensation, acknowledge it by mentally saying 'falling'. Observe the rising and falling sensations. When the mind becomes more focused, omit the words and stay focused on the rising and falling sensations. Should there be any drifting thoughts while you are focusing on your breathing, be aware of those thoughts and acknowledge them by saying the word 'thinking' three times in your head, or more if the thoughts linger on. If a smell or sound enters your nose or ears, be aware of them, too, and simply repeat to yourself 'smelling' or 'hearing' three times before bringing the focus back to the breathing again. A study by Creswell et al. showed that labelling sensations and thoughts helped to shift brain activity away from the emotional brain and instead towards the reasoning and attention area of the brain. This may explain why well-trained meditators react less to emotional impulses and have better attention spans, because their prefrontal cortex is regularly trained to become more focused, and their amygdala is less activated.

- When you are in bed, focus your attention on the sensation of your breathing, either through the nostrils or at an abdominal level. Make your out-breath as long as possible. Shift the focus of the mind from thinking to the awareness of the breath.

Breathe away negative thoughts and emotions

Acknowledge the negative thoughts and feelings as they occur without adding any judgement. No need to push them away. Breathe out long and slowly, and simply let go of your thoughts and feelings with your out-breath. All the time, be totally aware of your breath.

If you experience heaviness of heart, the following recommended breathing technique works quite well:

If your chest feels tight from all the worries, think of your heart, then take a short fast breath and direct it straight to the heart. Then breathe out quickly from your heart. Let your body drop as you let all the worries out of your heart and chest. Repeat a few times to get rid of the accumulated worries. Then you can continue with your meditation.

No excuse for not practising

The most common excuse people make for not practising meditation is that they don't have the time. As you can see, all you need to do is to breathe in and out – an everyday activity. Bring awareness to your breathing, and be mindful of it.

Notice how you breathe and how it affects your body. When your breathing is more steady and refined, your thoughts will subside, and your mind feels calmer. You can try it right now.

Meditating on the sensation of pain

Meditating in a sitting position for a lengthy period can lead to aches and pains. However, if you persevere, you will find that the aches and pains may disappear, move elsewhere, or intensify.

When you have been running for a long period of time, your muscles hurt, but when you go beyond the pain threshold, endorphins (a natural pain-killer) are released to relieve the pain. However, it is not advisable for beginners or the physically impaired to stretch themselves beyond what their bodies can handle. Try shorter sessions of sitting meditation each day and gradually increase the time period as you progress.

If the pain persists, you may like to try meditating on the sensation of pain. Look at the pain and acknowledge it by mentally saying 'aching, aching, aching'. If you keep looking at it without any judgement, you will notice that the pain moves. It is not constantly fixed in one location as one would expect. Like any other sensation, it comes and goes and it moves around. Notice how it starts and lingers and how long it lasts. Labelling the pain sensation may make the pain increase sharply at first but then subside. Fear of pain and the desire to get rid of it lead to a stress response, resulting in cortisol being released and muscles tensed-up. The pain sensation worsens. But when the mind is the watcher of the pain rather than being part of the pain, the intensity of the pain will be reduced. Often when the meditation is over, the pain immediately vanishes. This goes to show that we suffer more from fear of pain, making the pain more unbearable than it actually is.

Standing meditation

This technique gives you an alternative to sitting meditation, should you get tired of sitting. Don't change your postures too often too soon, as this can become disruptive, and you will lose your mindfulness and focus.

-    Stand in a comfortable position with your feet apart. Take a few deep breaths and gently allow the eyes to close. Focus your attention on your feet. Be aware of the sensation of your feet touching firmly on the ground. Then scan your body from your feet to the top of your head. Check whether there's any part of your body that still feels tense or stiff, relax them, and scan the body from the top of your head down to your feet.

-    If you feel giddy or fear that you might fall over, you can keep your eyes half-open, casting down on the floor a few feet ahead. Focus your attention on your breathing or the rising and falling sensation of the abdomen. If your mind begins to drift, bring it back to your breaths. You can practise this while waiting for the bus, queuing at a till, or anywhere.

-    Alternatively, you may also choose to breathe through your feet while standing. Of course, you still take in some air through your nose. However, as you breathe in, focus on the soles of your feet. Feel the air coming in through your feet, travelling up your legs, back, shoulders, and head. When you breathe out, direct the air down to your chest and let it out through your feet. This will help to relax you, because long, deep breaths have a positive effect on the parasympathetic nervous system.

-    You can also choose to focus your attention on the sensation of your feet touching the ground. Be aware of any sensations in your feet, such as the temperature or the texture of the ground underneath your feet. You may find that soon enough your feet start to ache. Normally, you can be on your feet for hours when you go window shopping, chatting to someone, or teaching, without any noticeable pain, because these activities distract you from the aching sensation. It's only when you shift the attention to your body that the pain becomes prominent. After 15 minutes of standing meditation, the pain may become more pronounced. Mindfully adjust your position, and the pain may subside temporarily. Or, you can mindfully shift your focus from your feet to your breath whilst remaining in a standing position. Before long, the pain may return. Look at the pain with a non-judgemental mind. Notice that the sensation is not a constant presence. It shifts. It comes and goes. This is how one develops wisdom to understand things as the way they are.

Walking meditation

The way you walk tells the state of mind you are in. We change the way we walk all day depending on how we feel, but we tend to have one tendency of the way we walk. According to *A Guide to Vipassana Practice* by Dhammadharo Bikkhu, there are three ways of walking: with anger, greed, or delusion. For example, do you walk with your heel down first, toes down first or do you walk with your feet going sideways?

If you walk with your heel down first, that's walking with the tendency towards anger. You will notice that when children don't get what they want, they stamp their feet – with the heels going down first. If it continues, you are likely to become a grumpy person! Most people walk with their heels down first. That's why we have a lot of stressed and irritated people around. By changing the way you walk, you can change the state of mind you are in.

If you walk with your toes down first, that's walking with the tendency towards greed. When you walk to the fridge, for example, or when you walk towards the item of your desire in a shop, you walk with your toes down first. If you walk with your feet going sideways like a duck, that's walking with delusion. When you do walking meditation, it is advisable to keep your feet straight and put each foot down flat-foot.

Standing and walking meditation can be practised together. You can do it in the office, walking up and down the corridor when you fetch your coffee or when you need a little break. There are many different methods of walking mediation. For example, you may choose to focus on your breathing while you walk, or you may focus on the sensation of your feet touching the ground, provided that you are mindful of every step. There is a fast walk and a slow walk. For the slow walk, focus on the movement of your feet. Find a space that you can walk back and forth at least ten paces each way, or an open space that you can walk through or in a circle. It is best practised bare foot, but, if not possible, you can wear socks.

-       Stand with your feet slightly apart, your right hand loosely rested on top of your left wrist. Cast your eyes downwards on the floor about a metre in front of you. Be mindful, and bring awareness to your posture. Always start with your right foot. Bring the attention to your right foot. As you lift your right heel, be aware of the sensation of the heel lifting. For instance, you may feel some cool air underneath. As you put your right foot forward, be mindful and make sure that your foot is parallel to the ground: not too high and not so low that it drags on the ground. When you place your foot flat on the ground, be fully aware of the sensation of your foot touching the solid or soft ground underneath. Do the same with your left foot and continue till you get to the end of your walking path. Put your left foot next to your right and practise standing meditation for a moment, being aware of the sensation of your feet on the ground, or focusing on deep breaths. Or, you can breathe in through your feet, breathing all the way to the top of your head, then breathe out through your feet. Do it three times. When you are ready to turn, be mindful of your turning motion. Your attention should be focused on the sensation of your feet turning. Make each movement very slow so you can be mindful throughout.

-       If you find that your mind starts drifting, know that this is normal. Simply bring your attention back to walking. One thing you can try is labelling your movements. Different schools of meditation have different labelling words. The one below is based on a three-step motion walking meditation – taught at the Buddhapadipa Temple in Wimbledon for the beginners' class. To keep your mind focused on the feet movements, you can label them as 'right/left-goes-thus'. Always start with the right foot and end with the left. On the word 'right', lift the heel of your right foot. Be aware of sensation underneath your right heel. On the word 'go', put your right foot forward and be aware of the sensation as you move your foot forward. On the word 'thus' put your foot firmly on the ground. Again, be aware of the sensation – this can be the soft texture of the carpet, the hard texture of the wooden floor, or a sense of solidity underneath your foot. Make sure that the labelling and the movements synchronise. If your foot goes faster or slower than the labelling, you are not in the present moment; rather you are in the past or the future. If the labelling corresponds with your action but your mind drifts off elsewhere, then you lack the awareness of the sensation. It's like the body is being put on auto-pilot. Chances are you will start wobbling. Do the same with your left foot – 'left-goes-thus'. Remain mindful and aware of every step.

-       When you come to the end of your walking path, stop. Slowly and mentally say to yourself 'standing', being fully aware of the sensation of your feet firmly touching on the ground. Do this three times. When you are ready to turn back, acknowledge it by mentally saying 'intending to turn' three times. Focus the attention on your right foot. Turn in a clockwise direction in three-step movements. Mentally say 'turning' as you mindfully lift your right foot and move it to the right, followed by your left, and be aware of the sensations of the movements throughout. Do it two more times. On the third turn you will be facing the path you are going to walk back.

-       Now say 'intending to walk' three times to yourself before proceeding to walk. Shift the attention to your right foot and continue with right goes-thus and left goes-thus. Discard the labelling once your mind becomes steadily focused.

For normal-speed walking meditation, focus chiefly on the sensation of your feet touching the ground. Alternatively, you can focus on breathing in and out whilst walking.

Lying down meditation

Scientists have found that practising meditation prior to sleep increases production of the sleep-aid hormone, melatonin. If you suffer from insomnia or have difficulty getting to sleep, you may like to meditate in bed before sleep.

You can focus on breathing in and out and make the out-breath longer than the in-breath while lying down on your back. Or, you can focus on the rising and falling sensations of the abdomen.

-       Another option you may choose is to breathe through your feet – the same technique as standing meditation except that you do it while lying down. Before you know it, you might nod off. In 2008 I conducted a small research project based on this method and found that it had a significant effect on menopausal sleeping problems.

Mindful eating

Eating is one of life's pleasures – a comfort for some and a favourite pastime for many. However, one tends to overeat when one's attention is not on eating itself but elsewhere on reading, thinking, working, or watching TV. When we are not fully conscious of the chewing, swallowing, or the taste of the food we are eating, there is no sense of satiety. Hence we are likely to eat more than needed. If we eat slowly and mindfully with each mouthful, we can taste the food better and we will eat less.

-   Give every eating activity your mindful attention. Be mindful of your hand lifting the food to your mouth, be aware of your mouth opening and closing, be aware of the chewing sensation and the taste: sweet, sour, salty…. Be mindful of whether you like or dislike or neither like nor dislike the taste before swallowing. You are fully aware of all relevant sensations with every spoonful. You may find, for example, that the liking sensation arises with the first few spoonsful of your favourite dish. After a few more, the degree of liking may diminish. The desire the carry on eating may also wane. This may sound tedious, but with practise you will eat just the right amount that your body needs. If you are drinking tea, be aware of your hand picking up the cup. You can even label the movement as lifting, lifting, lifting, and bending, bending, bending as you bend your arm to put the cup to your lips. When it touches your lips, you can acknowledge it by mentally saying touching, touching, touching. Observe all the sensations as the tea enters your mouth, the heat, the taste on your tongue, the warm sensation as it goes down your throat to your stomach.

-   If you are attached to a certain type of food, you may choose to contemplate on the nature of food consumption prior to eating. See the desirable food in front of you for what it actually is: once inside your body it will be mixed with saliva and stomach juices before going through the process of digestion. The end result is the same for all foods, regardless of how desirable they were in the first place.

Being in the present moment

When you are mindful, you are in the present moment with whatever you are doing. Whether you are working on a computer, cooking, or walking the dog, you are fully aware. Your mind doesn't dart here and there to give you a feeling of restlessness.

When a thought arises, be aware of it and any associated feelings that come with it – don't reject or act on it. Just be mindful; you will be able to learn from it: how it makes you feel, how it changes, and how long it lasts. With regular practise, the mind will eventually comes to recognise the pattern or characteristics of states of mind as well, for example, sadness or anger from beginning to end. Observe and understand them for what they actually are, and they will lose their significance, allowing the mind to let go. When you are mindful, the mind can't play tricks on you. It can't tempt you to dwell on the painful past as it used to.

Some may think that being aware of what one is doing/ thinking is a waste of time because nothing much is happening. What's the point of, for instance, being in the present moment with peeling an onion? When you are mindful, the mind does not go into the past or future but remains at peace right here, right now.

Another example is when an annoying person has left the room, you should feel relieved. Being unmindful and stuck in the immediate past, the mind follows that person out of the room. It wants to fix the annoying past to feel better. Your annoyance thus continues. Be mindful and keep the mind home within your body or on the task at hand. Only then will the duration of your agitation or negative moods shorten, allowing you to enjoy the present moment.

Applying mindfulness to daily life

We tend to let the mind do whatever it pleases. When the body needs a rest, the mind keeps going and sometimes pushes the body over the limit. It's going to take some time to train and discipline the mind. Try to apply mindfulness to your daily routine:

Before getting out of bed in the morning, spend a few minutes being mindful of your breathing. When you are about to get out of bed, know that you intend to get out of bed. Be mindful and fully aware of each movement you make, from raising your knees to rolling over to the side of the bed, sitting up and getting out of bed, and making the bed. Or, when you walk to the bathroom, be aware of the sensations in your feet. When you wash your face and brush your teeth, be in the present moment with your senses and actions. It isn't too difficult to be mindful of what you are doing, but maintaining this mindfulness is challenging, as there are too many distractions.

When you are mindful, your body and mind are in tune with each other. Mindfulness will stop the mind in its tracks from darting around, indulging in thinking and seasoning your thoughts, leaving you feeling more at peace and focused. You will sleep better and have more energy and your memory will be improved. Most importantly, you will be able to enjoy a healthier mind and body. As long as you continue with regular practise, mindfulness will transform your life!

8 Allowing the mind to let go and forgive

We all enjoy freedom of speech. At the same time, we need to watch how our spoken or written words and words we plan to say about others affect us from within. For example, when we condemn others, our mind is already and instantly agitated, and muddy. We bring the agitation into the mind, hold on to our disapproval of their wrong actions, and become unhappy. When this turns into a habit, our mind will not be at peace. As we get older, we may realise we should have let go of all these unnecessary agitations long time ago. Even when we have decided to let go, the upsetting past may soon return. The rational brain is telling us one thing, and the mind is doing another.

We cannot change our past, but we can do something now to make sure that the mind is not chained to the past and thus feel happier.

Wanting to let go and letting go

Wanting to let go and letting go are not the same. The former is the desire to do so; we think about doing it or wanting to forget it or pretending we don't care so that we don't have to suffer the emotional pain. This doesn't work, because the mind understands nothing. The process of letting go comes naturally when the mind understands what it is doing and thinking, allowing us to make peace with the past. Without making peace, there is more pain:

Twenty-one-year-old Ella was asked by her parents, who were living overseas, to make regular visits to her grandma in a small village. Ella wanted to spend more time with her boyfriend so she refused. The fact that she was spending time with a man her father regarded as 'unsuitable' rather than being a loving, obedient granddaughter infuriated her father. Harsh words were exchanged. Ella slammed down the phone. She refused to answer any more calls from her parents. She married that boyfriend, and her parents weren't invited to the wedding. Both sides were waiting for an apology. Ella's mum tried to offer a truce. Her efforts did not receive a warm welcome. Ella clung onto her anger, and her father had held on to his hurt. They both missed out on ten years of a father-daughter relationship because of one small incident and spent ten years in silence.

One way of making peace with the past is to realise that this suffering can happen to anybody at any time; it's not personal. In today's competitive world, this realisation helps us to be kinder to one another:

Every morning, village people pushed and jostled each other to squeeze in to crowded buses to get to work in the city. Stressed and grumpy, they shouted unpleasant words at each other. Then came a big flood. Their village was submerged in nearly two metres of water, with many losing their homes and loved ones. Some suffered from skin diseases from wading through the dirty flood water; food and drinking water were in short supply. After a month of flooding, the same people were still waiting to go to work at the same bus stop. This time, nobody was pushing. Instead, each insisted on offering seats to young children and the elderly: they didn't seem to mind waiting for the next bus in the dirty water. They smiled to each other and spoke with kind words. They realised that their individual needs meant nothing. A lot of what they once had was destroyed in the flood, but what they had gained was a true sense of community. They have now developed friendships in the face of adversity and show care and kindness towards each other – the important human qualities for humanity to progress.

Letting go of others' mistakes means being kind to oneself. It is also helpful to develop consideration and understanding/

acceptance of others' faults, therefore freeing our mind from unnecessary pain and suffering.

Dawn and Mark had frequent rows, stemming from his one night of infidelity. Mark apologised and tried his best to rectify the situation and save his marriage. Dawn kept referring to the past. Mark found it difficult to return home to a suspicious, angry wife. The door to her heart remained shut. As time went by, they no longer thought of themselves as a couple but rather 'it's you, it's me'. They disagreed on everything from childcare, finances, and holidays to minor things such as how to stack the dirty dishes. When Mark passed away, Dawn sank into depression. They both endured 20 years of unhappy marriage because she could not forgive him nor could she acknowledge the better side of him.

Fear and worry together with ego and identity can hinder the process of letting go.

Fear

What we fear most, when it comes to letting go, is losing our control. Will it make us look weak? Will others do whatever they want if we just let go? Will they treat us badly again? Blinded by fear, the mind clings to the familiar and is unable to experience the freedom from letting go.

Have you tried to rescue an insect from drowning by offering it something to climb onto? At first, it may reject your help. Faced with no other choice, it will reluctantly crawl onto whatever you offered. When you try to release it on safe ground, it shows more reluctance. Certain animals' first reaction to a helping hand can be that of aggression due to fear and distrust. Some can even become temporarily immobilised due to shock.

Our instinctive reaction to threatening situations may resemble that of animals' – fear of change and distrust of the unknown, hence an inability to let go. Letting go takes courage. Following a nasty fall, an elderly person may be scared of getting back on their feet again, and so try to stay in bed all day. The longer they stay in bed for fear of falling, the more their muscles will weaken, putting them at risk of further accidents. Fear of emotional pain can intensify the pain itself. Pluck up the courage to let go of unreasonable fear. What you gain is freedom, and it's empowering!

Worry

When people get serious injuries or illnesses, some lie in bed worrying about all kinds of unfortunate things instead of letting themselves get a good rest. They feel much worse because of their thoughts, and their immunity plummets due to stress. When we worry, we waste the opportunity to be happy right here right now.

Ego and identity

Often we identify with problems, people, things, and events as if they were extensions of ourselves, thinking of them in terms of my problem, my partner, my children, my house, my country … And because they are all 'ours', we can't let go. We even develop a dislike towards the other person who opposes or strongly disagrees with us or our loved ones. Whatever that person does becomes agitating because of our bias. In reality, all we cling to is part of nature, and we have no absolute control over any of these things, be they our loved ones, pets, homes, possessions, health, etc.

Holding on to the past, our views become like a pool of stagnant water. Every time our dissatisfaction arises, it is dumped into this pool, polluting it even more and, in due course, forming unpleasant habits and tendencies. It only takes a little something to upset us and our dormant tendencies flare up. An apology will clear the air, heal the pain, and give you both a chance to make peace with the past and move on. An apology can be from an individual, an organisation, a country, or a government. If you have done something hurtful or harmful to someone, why not take this opportunity to let go of your pride and apologise to them now? Don't let pride and ego stand in the way. What are these pride and ego anyway? In this context, they are merely thoughts and negative emotions that we cling to.

Forgiving

Whatever you dislike or hate will always be with you; they live on in your mind, stalking you like a shadow. It's better to forgive, let go, off-load such emotional burden, and experience the sweet taste of freedom. Like lavender crushed between fingers, it bears no harm but continues to give out the delightful, sweet fragrance – we should strive to bring out the positive side.

A study by Whited et al. showed that apologies help people forgive and let go of their anger faster and therefore reduce their cardiovascular activity, which could potentially be harmful for their health otherwise. Not that it's hard to say sorry, but we tend to be coy saying it. To make it easier for everybody to apologise and forgive one another and increase the GNH (Gross National Happiness) index, perhaps we should establish a National or an International Apology Day so that we can all apologise at personal level, national and international level without fear of losing face and clear the air once a year!

Letting go process works best when you also generate loving kindness toward others.

Negative thought energy

Nobody can see or know what we are thinking, but our message can still be picked up on an unconscious level, and it can boomerang back to us.

Whilst stuck in a long queue at the check-out, Vicky was getting anxious about running late for her appointment. The staff at the till were chatting and joking with each customer as well as with each other – ignoring the fact that the queue was long and some customers were in a hurry. As Vicky's appointment drew nearer, her annoyance with the check-out staff increased. She suggested that the store put more people on the till. Her plea fell on deaf ears. Angry words popped up in her head like fireworks and she found herself directing these thoughts towards the smiley check-out lady who would be serving her. When it was her turn to be served, the smiles from the check-out lady ceased. She became grumpy for no apparent reason. No words were spoken as she threw Vicky's carefully selected items into a bag. She didn't seem to care whether the fruits would be bruised. Vicky was startled by her abrupt change of behaviour. When it was all done, she continued to serve other customers with friendliness and smiles. Vicky only realised afterwards that her negative signals were duly returned!

So if we want to give off the vibes, make sure that they are positive. Loving kindness is a highly beneficial, positive thought energy that you can send to others to bring harmony and peace – not just to yourself but to others as well.

Loving kindness

Loving kindness means having goodwill for all beings and wishing them well regardless of who they are. For those who have a tendency towards getting angry, this exercise is highly recommended.

How to send loving kindness?

Before you send loving kindness to others, you need to send it to yourself first. When you are kind to yourself, you will not harm yourself by indulging in negative thoughts or holding on to grudges. When there is kindness in your heart, it will pour out naturally towards others.

Simply close your eyes, take a deep, deep breath, think of yourself, and say the words 'May I be happy' in your head and breathe out. Send it from the centre of your chest to all parts of your body and feel a sense of love and kindness spreading throughout. Do it a few times until you can feel it in every part of your body.

Sending loving kindness to others

The next step is to send loving kindness to those closest to you, such as your family and friends. Breathe in and think of these people, see their faces in front of you or say their names in your head, and wish them happiness and well-being. Say 'May you all be happy!' and breathe out. Send the loving kindness to them as you exhale, and do it with heartfelt conviction. Do it every day, and you may be surprised by the results: people who you meet in the street may smile at you for no reason; those who hadn't been nice to you before may change their tune! Send loving kindness to all beings, alive or dead.

Sending loving kindness to your rivals

It is equally important to send loving kindness to those you dislike, those you are envious of, and those you don't get on with. It's more difficult to send loving kindness to someone who has hurt you. One lady said to me that she had problems sending it to her ex-husband because she still felt strong animosity towards him and didn't want him to be happy because of 'all the hell' he put her through. This is understandable. However, those negative feelings she holds towards him can continue to make her feel unhappy, keeping her in the past and preventing her from moving forward.

The importance of sending loving kindness

Firstly, it reminds you to be kind to yourself – both body and mind. Often we tend to be unkind towards ourselves by indulging in food intake, depriving ourselves of sleep, thinking negative thoughts, and harming the body with drugs and intoxicants. We tend to ignore the body that serves us so until it becomes ill. So it brings a healthy attitude towards oneself.

Secondly, sending loving kindness can free one's heart from negativity, anger, and hatred. You might have to do it grudgingly for your rivals at first, but after a while, you will find that you feel better about yourself and are able to forgive them much faster. Generate loving kindness with compassion. Let it come from your heart. You may wonder 'Why should I wish this nasty person any happiness at all when I feel like punching them?' The point is that nasty people are not happy in themselves. That's why they behave unkindly to others. By sending them loving kindness, you may be helping them to become a more caring person.

Thirdly, even if you have to force yourself to wish your rivals well, your intention to send loving kindness to others will make you feel better in the long run. It will fill your heart with a positive attitude, and people will be attracted to your positivity. By generating good feelings, you will become happier. Those who give tend to be happier than those who receive. Most importantly, sending loving kindness will help you to let go of your anger and resentment towards others, allowing you to forgive them. You may not see an immediate result after you have done it, but keep trying. You may be surprised by the positive changes.

How to know if the loving kindness arrived?

You won't know whether your dead relatives or your pets have received your loving kindness, but for the receivers who are still alive, you may notice some positive changes in their behaviour, whether it's a few more smiles from your boss, a compliment from a neighbour, or just a relaxation in the tension between you and a work rival.

When best to send loving kindness?

You can send it at any time, and the more the better. However, you need to have kindness in order to generate it. A simple act of kindness like giving up your seat on the train, helping an old lady reach for an item in the supermarket, giving money to a homeless person … or when you see reports of some atrocity on TV and you feel the urge to help those who are suffering, at that moment kindness is blossoming in your heart. Why not send those well-wishing thoughts to them, or do something to help? You can also send loving kindness straight after praying or meditating. When your mind is calm, your communications to others become clearer and more effective.

Before you leave the house, send loving kindness to those you will come into contact with that day. Send it to all beings before you go to sleep. Reduce your anxiety before a job interview by sending loving kindness to the interviewers. It doesn't matter if you have never met them, send it just the same. Having an argument with your partner, parents, or children? Send loving kindness to them. Wish for them all to be well and happy!

Many people have told me how surprised they were to see positive changes in the people they sent loving kindness to. People whom they fell out with became nicer; people who always gave them problems became more supportive. Some felt a sense of emotional release. Some haven't witnessed any obvious changes in others, but at least they are taking an initial step towards forgiveness, which helps to reduce their own stress. The more envious you are of your colleague's big bonus the more loving kindness you need to send. You can then be happy for them rather than giving them a fake smile whilst sending out an envious vibe that they can detect. Generate positive feelings in your heart and send them out to counteract your own negativity and negative vibes you receive from others. Make a habit of sending loving kindness to everybody, regardless. Send it to people out there who you've never met, to those in crisis, to those who you are going to meet, have already met, or will never see again. You'll find that you get on better with people and are more in harmony with your environment.

Send loving kindness, forgive, and…. let go!

Conclusion

and taking action

Here are some reminders of what we've talked about throughout the book:

• Know your triggers.

• Watch your arising thoughts, feelings, and emotions that correspond to those triggers without seasoning any of them.

• Use the 'thinking, thinking, thinking' mantra to help you counteract the arising thoughts.

• Beware of liking and disliking.

• Know that nothing lasts forever, including the issues that are troubling you.

• Thoughts, feelings and emotions come and go. They have no substance that you should hold onto. See them for what they actually are, and let them go.

• Look at things from every perspective rather than through singular tunnel vision.

• Contemplate the delusional perception of 'me, mine, and self'.

• Live in the present moment. Enjoy this very moment. Don't wait for something to happen to be happy.

• Watch your anger from beginning to end rather than spreading it.

• Be kind to yourself. Forgive, forgive, and forgive and let go – for the sake of your healthy heart and healthy mind.

• Accept reality – that that's the way things are.

• Send loving kindness every day.

• Meditate. Be mindful of what you are doing, thinking, and saying.

Taking action

Now it's time to take action to tame that restless mind. For that, you need to set up your goals and work at it to achieve the objectives you want. Without goal setting and determination to see it through, nothing will materialise. If we keep postponing, we are likely to give up on the whole idea.

Note down what you want to achieve within the next few weeks, in a month's time, or in a year. Remember, once you've set your goals, you need to stick to them, and give them your best shot; otherwise, they are not going to work. What are your specific targets? How would you like things to change, given that the triggers may remain the same? For example, you may want to be able to handle your children's demands better without losing your temper; or you may want to deal with a difficult colleague in a calmer manner; or you'd like to be less angry when things don't go your own way.

1. Make a list below of the negative habitual reactions that you may have and how you would tame your mind. Be as specific as you can. For example:

- Next time I get irritated with loud noise next door, I will look at my emotion from beginning to end.

- From now on I am going to be mindful when eating so that I won't overeat too often.

2. How keen are you? Very, average, not sure? If you are not keen enough, then you will need to find some inspiration or motivation to get started.

3. What would stop you from taking the action? Note down these constraints and be aware of them when they try to distract or deter you from your commitment.

Your objectives must be realistic. If your objective is to never get angry or irritated again, then this may not work. A more realistic target is to become less angry or less irritable when under stress. You can aim at changing certain negative reactions or behaviours, but you need to give yourself enough time for the change to gradually take place. Do not expect an overnight transformation. If you have a strong tendency to get angry, you may aim at reducing your angry reaction within a few weeks or a month – provided that you practise mindfulness regularly.

Once you have set your goals, you will need to work at it, applying the methods in this book to make sure you reach the set targets. Commitment and motivation are crucial. After all, it has taken you months or year or your entire lifetime to develop some of those negative stress responses. They are not going to disappear within a day or two. You may feel better soon after practising some of the techniques in this book, but this does not guarantee a long-lasting effect unless you keep at it and make a habit of it. There's a saying: Nothing comes easy except for growing toenails. Hence you need to commit..

Your commitment

1.When are you planning to start doing it? (right now, this evening, today, tomorrow) Write down a couple of methods in this book you want to use/will be able to apply to your daily routine, and stick to them. Be specific about what methods you'll be using at work, when eating, walking home, waiting at the train station, before bed, etc. List as many routines as you can apply.

For example, you might like to do breathing meditation while sitting on the train on the way to and from work; or you may want to do walking meditation every time you fetch your coffee; or you will breathe through your feet when lying in bed. Or, you will try to look at your thoughts and feelings. Remember that the sooner you start, the better the result. If you procrastinate, you may not get started at all.

2. It is important that you practise regularly every day and stick to your goal at least for the first 3–4 weeks to allow it to work. If possible, let your friends or family know of your plan. Once you have told them, you will stick to your words and your practice.

3. Motivation is important. You may want to set up regular group sessions for certain activities such as sitting or walking meditation to avoid the monotony of doing it on your own. Make it fun. Are there any friends who might be interested in joining you? Note down their names. Perhaps, you can do walking meditation in a quiet park together.

Another thing you can do is to have a discussion group every once in a while. Each member can put forward their stressful issue in a bowl (name withheld) before the session. To ensure this is completely anonymous, their problems should be typed and put in same-size envelopes. Then the group can discuss how each would approach or deal with those troublesome situations.

Try to apply approaches you have read in this book. The outcome is not meant to be a resolution, but the exercise is to help you see things from different and broader perspectives on the situation that might be bothering you and to provide you with points of view which you might have overlooked. End your session with sending loving kindness.

If you have a discussion before a meditation session, make sure that you all do the deep breathing exercise prior to meditation. Breathe out any issues that might linger in your mind post-discussion and proceed to meditation. Do the same if you have a discussion following meditation. End every session with sending loving kindness. Let the loving kindness permeate every part of you. And send it to others, including the person whose problem the group discussed earlier.

Now you are all set.

The opportunity to succeed in taming your truant mind lies in your hands.

Your commitment can make it a reality.

Good luck – and may the present moment be with you!

References
and recommended reading

Journals

Creswell JD, Way BM, Eisenberger NI, Lieberman MD (2007) "Neural correlates of dispositional mindfulness during affect labelling", Psychosomatic Medicine, 69(6):560-5

Grewen KM, Girdler SS, Amico J, Light KC (2005) "Effects of partner support on resting oxytocin, cortisol, norepinephrine, and blood pressure before and after warm partner contact", Psychosomatic Medicine, 67(4): 531-8

Leiberman MD, Eisenberger NI, Crockett MJ et al (2007) "Putting feelings into words: affect labelling disrupts amygdala activity response to effective stimuli", Psychological Science, 18(5):421-8

Marazziti D, Canale D (2004) "Hormonal changes when falling in love", Psychoneuroendocrinology, 29(7):931-6

Matud P (2004) "Gender differences in stress and coping style", Personality and Individual Differences, 37(7): 1401-1405

Taylor SE, Klein LC, Lewis BP et al (2000) "Biobehavioral responses to stress in females: Tend-and-befriend not fight-or-flight", Psychological Review, 107, 411-429

Whited MC, Wheat AL, Larkin KT (2010) "The influence of forgiveness and apology on cardiovascular reactivity and recovery in response to mental stress", Journal of Behavioural Medicine, 33(4):293-304

Younger J, Aron A, Parke, S, Chaterjee N, Mackey S (2010) "Viewing pictures of a romantic partner reduces experimental pain: involvement of neural reward systems", PLOS ONE, 5 (10): e 13309

Books

Aamodt S, Wang S, *Welcome to Your Brain: The Science of Jet Lag, Love and Other Curiosities of Life*, Rider Books: London, 2008

Austin JH, *Zen and the Brain*, The MIT Press: Cambridge, Massachusetts, US, 1999

Byrom T, The Dhammapada: *The Sayings of the Buddha*, Random House, Inc: New York, 1976

Dhammadharo Bikkhu, *A Guide to Vipassana Practice: The Four Postures*, published in Thai by The Vipassana Meditation Centre, Srai-ngam Dhammadararama Temple, Supanburi, Thailand

de Saint-Exupéry A, *The Little Prince*, translated by Katherine Woods, Pan Books Ltd, London 1974

Sapolsky RM, *Why Zebras Don't Get Ulcers*, Owl Books, Henry Holt and Company, LLC: New York, 2004

Ven. Pannapadipo P, *Vipassana Meditation: A Course for Beginners,* The Buddhapadipa Temple, produced by The Lay Buddhist Association, London

Ven. Gavesako M, *The Seven Practices for a Healthy Mind*, The Maya Gotami Foundation: Bangkok, Thailand, 2005

Other

Evans K, Can mindfulness meditation restore verbal memory in menopausal women?, MSc dissertation, Roehampton University, London, 2008

Further information

If you are interested in learning mindfulness meditation, the following places offer mindfulness teaching. Some are free, though donations are welcome and at some places there are charges for a longer retreat.

Great Britain

Buddhapadipa Temple, 14 Calonne Road, London SW19 5HJ, Tel: 020 8946 1357. Free meditation classes for beginners every Tuesday and Thursday from 7pm to 9pm and Saturday and Sunday from 4pm to 6pm. No need to book, just turn up.

Oxford Buddha Vihara, 356-358 Abingdon Rd, Oxford OX1 4TQ, Tel: 01865 791591

Amaravati Buddhist Monastery, St Margarets, Great Gaddesden, Hemel Hempstead HP1 3BZ, Tel: 01442 842455

Hartridge Buddhist Monastery, Upottery, Honiton, Devon EX14 9QE, Tel: 01404 891251

Thailand

Most Thai temples offer free meditation classes, though donations are very much appreciated. For a longer retreat there may be a small fee to cover food, electricity and water.

Not all temples offer meditation teaching in English and some only offer it at certain times of the year so it is important to check time and availability in advance.

The following website has details of temples all over Thailand where you can learn meditation in English: http://www.dhammathai.org/e/meditation/page26.php

20156740R00073

Printed in Great Britain
by Amazon